Divine Interventions

My Personal Story

Alan Dean

World rights reserved. This book or any portion thereof may not be copied or reproduced in any form or manner whatever, except as provided by law, without the written permission of the publisher, except by a reviewer who may quote brief passages in a review.

This book is sold with the understanding that the publisher is not engaged in giving spiritual, legal, medical, or other professional advice. If authoritative advice is needed , the reader should seek the counsel of a competent professional.

Copyright © 2013 Aspect Books
ISBN-13: 978-1-4796-0081-6 (Paperback)
ISBN-13: 978-1-4796-0082-3 (ePub)
ISBN-13: 978-1-4796-0083-0 (Kindle / Mobi)
Library of Congress Control Number: 2012923341

All scripture quotations are taken from
the King James Version Bible.

Published by

Dedication

I want to dedicate this book to my dear wife who has been the wind beneath my wings for 40 plus years and also to all the persons mentioned herein who helped make these divine interventions possible.

Table of Contents

Chapter 1	God Manifesting Himself	7
Chapter 2	Blessings of Divine Interventions	10
Chapter 3	Experiencing Divine Interventions	16
Chapter 4	My Growing Up Years	20
Chapter 5	A Turn in My Life	25
Chapter 6	Discouragement to Joy	29
Chapter 7	My Introduction to Adventists	33
Chapter 8	God's Hand Over Me	38
Chapter 9	Accepting Jesus As My Saviour	47
Chapter 10	A Big Step	51
Chapter 11	A New Direction	59
Chapter 12	A Miracle Bakery	65
Chapter 13	God Leads in the Farm Purchase	72
Chapter 14	A New Broader Venture	75
Chapter 15	A New Calling	80
Chapter 16	Entering Pastoral Ministry	88

Chapter 17	Joys as a Pastor	97
Chapter 18	Retired—Really?	106
Chapter 19	A New Challenge	116
Chapter 20	Closing Thoughts	124

Chapter 1

God Manifesting Himself

By the time one retires and is still of a sound mind, I believe everyone should sit down, relax, and ponder what life has taught him. What words of wisdom and experience has he gained that might be of value to other people. Life is full of ups and downs, out of which we gain blessings that God uses to increase our faith in Him and to remind us that we can not go it alone. Everyone's life is distinctly different, just as we were created uniquely different. But we are also all humans with similar challenges and needs. God intends for us to be a support and encouragement to one another, so that we might all win the race for eternal life.

It's also good to look over our years to see how God has intervened in our life. God surely purposes to do so. It's not just to give guidance and help through our life, but also to manifest Himself to us in a personal way so that we might come to know Him and love Him. In John 17:3 Jesus states that eternal life is coming to know the only true God and Jesus Christ whom He has sent. God wants us all to be saved, so He designs divine interventions in our lives so that we might see and experience our God of love, wisdom, and power.

We know that God manifests Himself abundantly through His Word. In it is the harmonious truth about God written over a period of 1600 hundred years. The Bible is filled with situations when God made Himself known to individuals and nations by giving them direction, admonition, and help. Jesus, of course, was the perfect manifestation of God in the Bible. In Him we see God's love and truth personified because He was God who had come to earth. Our faith grows as we behold His life and His sacrificial love for us on the cross. Our hope for today and tomorrow is in Jesus.

Nature also reflects our Creator God. The lessons we can see and learn from nature are endless, just as from the Bible. We can come to know God as the awesome Creator that He is. From the start, everything He made was "very good" and perfect. Today God still shines through the myriad of plants and animals and in the heavens above. They each declare His power and majesty. Each season of the year paints a different love picture of God. All was designed that we might come to know our Lord and Saviour.

God loves us to the highest degree because we are created in His image. It's like we are a part of Him. Adam and Eve were a son and daughter to Him. And by accepting Jesus as our Saviour, we are again elevated to sons and daughters of God. We, too, can exclaim: "What manner of love the Father has bestowed upon us!" 1 John 3:1

For us to be so elevated, we must see the true picture of God, not the God we see depicted in our fallen world and fallen churches. We must go back to diligent Bible study with prayer and also be students of nature. I've studied nature enough to be awed by its beauty and complexity. Forestry was my field of study in college, and it has solidified my belief in our Creator God. But it was through the Bible that I found the Saviour. It's so true that "the goodness of God leadeth thee to repentance" (Romans 2:4).

Another method I want to mention by which God manifests

Himself to us is through spiritual music. Music is as much a part of God as are the visible things created. Job 38:7 points out that there were joy and singing in heaven when our world was created. Singing and music were a big part of worship and daily life of the Hebrews. And I have read that Jesus would sing while He worked in the carpenter shop. In the Upper Room Jesus led out in a joyful hymn of praise before they all left for Gethsemane. The 144,000 have a special song of victory they sing in heaven. Surely all heaven enjoys music and singing. It draws them closer to God.

David sensed that music would please his Lord when he prepared to move the ark of God to Jerusalem. Chapters 15 and 16 of 1st Chronicles describes the joy, singing, and music that accompanied this grand occasion. The Levites, gifted in music, were appointed to be the singers as they played their different special musical instruments. Oh, if we Christians could incorporate more of this truly spiritual music in our worship, we would be blessed as these Israelites were that day.

God has given special gifts of singing and music to people all through history. And through their talents He has drawn many people to Him. David was a master of this art. It's too bad that the music to the psalms wasn't preserved along with the psalms. His son, Solomon, used plenty of praise music in the temple dedication (2 Chronicles 7:6,7) which I'm sure lifted everyone to God's higher plane. Many people today have very busy schedules, but even a short amount of nice spiritual music will change the mood for hours. Have some of your favorite CDs available for listening at mealtime, in the living room, and in the car. Jesus wants to lift you up!

Chapter 2

Blessings of Divine Interventions

As wonderful as the Bible, nature, and music are to manifest our loving God to us earthlings, I believe there is a 4th way that is even more wonderful and effective. And that is through personal divine interventions. Times when He chooses to break into our life in some unique, special fashion. Sometimes it may be to rescue us from a danger, often through our bad decisions. We've all had an experience on the highway, on the job, or elsewhere when God sent his angel to prevent a tragedy. In His doing this, we come to greatly appreciate His constant abiding presence.

Sometimes God breaks into our life through answers to prayer, maybe for healing, guidance, encouragement, or some other need. I remember praying for the neighbor lady across our street who was suffering from neuropathy, and had been for years. One Sabbath afternoon her husband asked me to pray specifically for God to heal her. We both prayed that day. The next morning she was healed of this ailment and has been ever since. This occurred very shortly after I met them, and has been a bonding experience between us. But it has also been a bonding experience between God and me.

But the most awesome divine interventions seem to happen when people step out in faith to follow God and His plan for them. It might be to do a special work for God that is beyond their capability. Missionaries often step out in faith in this way. But people do it when they sense a clear calling from God. They don't know how it will be accomplished, but they know that they and God can do it together. They understand that "with God all things are possible". (Matt.19:26)

There are many examples in the Bible (and since that time) where people have stepped out in faith to follow the Lord. And in every case God blessed them with divine interventions to bring about success. And by doing this, these individuals came to know Him better and their faith grew. God is ever looking for ways to increase our faith because it is through our faith that we are saved by His grace.

Early in Bible history Abraham stepped out in faith to follow God when he was called to leave his homeland, relatives, and friends and go to a land yet unknown to him. And Abraham was blessed with many divine interventions and an intimacy with God that few people have attained. James 2:23 states that Abraham "was called the Friend of God". Isn't that an amazing relationship for one to attain? But Jesus said that relationship can be ours too. In John 15:14,15 Jesus says that as we come to know God and love Him and His commandments, we too become His friends, not servants.

Moses too comes to mind. He certainly stepped out in faith (with some urging from God) to return to Egypt and lead the Israelites out of their captivity. Even to get Moses' initial attention, God made a miraculous divine intervention at a burning bush that wasn't being consumed. This miracle was to show Moses that this was the only true God that was speaking to him. See Exodus 3:2-6.

Moses felt too small for such a big calling. But after God personally answered all his excuses, Moses finally set out for Egypt (then the most powerful nation on earth) in faith that God and he were going to deliver the Israelites from bondage and go to the Promised Land. The Lord's divine interventions continued one after another. First God sent the 10 plagues which convinced, not only Pharaoh, but all Egypt and Israel that Moses' God was all-powerful and that He meant business. Pharaoh finally agrees that Israel can leave. This was still a hard decision for him because a lot of work in the empire would have to go undone after they left. The Israelites were good, hard-working slaves.

This was the main reason that Pharaoh changed his mind a few days later and went after the Israelites to bring them back. But as we know, God divinely intervenes in that plan there at the Red Sea. He rescues His people and drowns Pharaoh and his army. God used this miracle (saved from the brink of disaster) to manifest Himself as a God that they could trust. This is a key reason for divine interventions: that we might learn to trust Him more and trust ourselves less. Solomon says it so nicely: "Trust in the Lord with all thine heart; lean not unto thine own understanding. In all thy ways acknowledge Him, and He shall direct thy paths". (Proverbs 3:5,6)

Another reason for divine interventions is to assure us that He can provide for our personal needs, even under seemingly hopeless situations. As the Israelites entered the wilderness, they discovered that food and good water could be scarce, especially for their size group of around one million people. But they were to learn that this is no problem for God. Water could be made pure by felling a tree into the lake (Exodus 15) and gotten from a rock when there was no water (Exodus 17). Food could be sent from heaven in the form of manna, an all-purpose food (Exodus 16). Though Israel still often stumbled in faith, the manna continued regularly for 40 years. God continued to manifest Himself until a faithful generation was ready to be taken into the Promised Land. Gaining confidence in God took time, but God patiently bore with them and continued to show His trustworthiness. Through these 40 years Moses, too, gained a very close relationship with God because he had stepped out in faith.

Truly God "is able to do exceeding abundantly above all that we ask or think according to the power that worketh in us". (Ephesians 3:20) As our Saviour, God is able to do (and has done) the miraculous for our salvation as well. Jesus is able "to make reconciliation for the sins of the people (all people) for He Himself hath suffered being tempted, He is able to succour (help) them that are tempted". (Hebrews 2:18) And finally, Jude 24 adds that Jesus "is able to keep you from falling and to present you faultless before the presence of His glory with exceeding joy".

Yes, God wants to show Himself able in every circumstance to provide for our every physical and spiritual need. God proved this in amazing ways through the life of Jesus on this earth, beginning with His incarnation through Mary and the Holy Spirit. This divine intervention (Jesus becoming human) is truly beyond our understanding. For this very reason, many today don't believe in Christ's miraculous birth. But we don't need to understand every divine intervention. We are only to believe.

Jesus showed his divinity in many ways through His healing and teaching. In John 7:32 the Pharisees and the chief priests sent officers to arrest Jesus. But they returned later without Him. In John 7:45 they ask the officers why they came back without Him. Their answer in verse 46 was "never man spake like this man". Jesus' divinity showed in the very words He spoke.

Jesus loved to manifest His divinity to people who expressed simple, blind faith in Him. His mother Mary expressed this faith at the wedding feast in Cana at the beginning of Jesus' ministry. She knew Jesus could resolve the shortage of the wine that had arisen (John 2:3-5). Jesus changed water into wine (non-alcoholic) as an answer to Mary's faith in Him. (verses 7-10)

Jesus responded similarly to Gentiles and to Jews who expressed faith in Him. Both the Roman centurian (Matthew 8:5-13) and the Syrophenician woman (Mark 7:24-30) expressed faith in Jesus and as a result had a loved one divinely healed by Him. In most all of Jesus' healings, others were present and could also receive the spiritual blessings of the divine interventions.

We too are meant to receive spiritual blessings (increased faith) from the divine interventions that we read in the Bible. If we imagine ourselves in their situation, we might find them most inspirational. Paul states in 1 Corinthians 10:11 that Bible experiences are written for our admonition (and instruction). Have you ever imagined yourself as someone in the Bible? Maybe one of the 12 disciples, and then thought about what life must have been like with Jesus. Think about not only the highlights that we can read about, but think what the day-to-day life with Jesus would be like.

Picture the meal times, the long walks all over Judea, the "in-house" every day talk, the personal talks with Jesus (on personal questions), and the cold, heat, and the rain. It's good to imagine all the rigors that Jesus went through for us. At the end of John's gospel he says "and there are many other things which Jesus did, which if they should be written everyone, I suppose that even the world itself could not contain the books that should be written". So we are left with plenty of room to imagine about the 33 years Jesus spent on this earth.

By doing so God may well give you some divine inspiration about the life of Jesus that will increase your faith in Him. Luke 18:8 states that faith in God is what Jesus is looking for when He comes again, a faith that reveals itself in works of mercy and obedience to His commands. And so, divine interventions are meant to increase our faith, which can be described as our trust in, our appreciation of, and our commitment to Jesus. I love to read about divine interventions that others have had. They seem to take away temptations to follow the world. At least for the moment, we only want to follow Jesus. Listen to the experiences of missionaries and evangelists and see if your faith doesn't take a jump.

Chapter 3

Experiencing Divine Interventions

The purpose here is to inspire you to seek divine interventions in your life. It is so much more powerful when we personally receive them. The highest experience you can have that will increase your faith is having personal, real interventions by the Lord in your life. It is then that you will see your faith grow by multiplication. And there is a way we can encourage such experiences to happen to us. It is called "stepping out in faith". We've already discussed how others have been blessed by doing so, but I want you to consider how you might step out in faith and make it a life-changing turn in your life.

First you might think of a work or a lifestyle change that God has already been putting in your mind that you should do, but you keep procrastinating because you don't feel you can do it. You may have a dozen reasons why you "can't", but this may be the very thing that He wants you to step out in faith to do. I've been in similar situations (and procrastinated) but then I remember that when God calls us, He enables us. So, by God's grace, I was able to move forward in faith.

I especially remember when, shortly after becoming a Christian, I was invited to join the literature evangelist work in Virginia. This is a special door-to-door work of sharing Jesus in the home, encouraging personal Bible study, selling Christian literature, and praying with people. I was at that time helping a church member on his dairy farm. The regional literature evangelist leader, Bob, attended the same church we did in Wytheville, VA and he would often ask me how soon I would be ready to join the team. I kept telling him "it wasn't for me" or "I would go broke doing that". But he and the Lord (and my wife) kept urging me to step out in faith and God would provide.

One day I decided that I really wasn't serving the Lord where I was and that I must step out in faith. That became the biggest life-changing decision I ever made. The devil worked hard to keep me from making that decision. If I hadn't, I don't really know where my life would have gone. All I know is that I did and my walk with God has been strong ever since. In a later chapter I want to share some of the divine interventions that occurred during my time in this work. Stepping out in faith allows God to come into your life to do things you couldn't do by yourself, and thus God gets the glory.

So if you, too, have been saying "No" to God about doing a work for Him because you feel inadequate, too old, too young, too poor, too busy, or whatever, think about the great resources of God that are at your disposal. He can supply whatever you feel you lack. And you will have the most enjoyable, spiritually rewarding time of your life. It may be a struggle at times, but you will see that the Lord always provides, sometimes in the most remarkable ways. And your faith will grow by leaps and bounds.

Maybe the Lord hasn't been reminding you of a work you should be doing, or at least you haven't heard it. This may be the time that you need to ask the Lord what new work, what higher step, He would like you to take. Remember that our spiritual life should be a growing experience. Someone has said "if we're not growing, we are dying; there's nothing in between". The Lord's plan is to give us "life more abundant" (John 10:10). Unless you are convinced you are where the Lord wants you (and this may be true of many), I suggest that you earnestly pray about your life and your service for the Lord. He may truly have something better for you.

If it's not a change in your work, it may be a change in your lifestyle that the Lord has in mind for you. This, too, needs to be on an upward scale. Sin and pollution are ever increasing. The lifestyle our parents or grandparents had isn't necessarily what we need today. But changing from Grandma's good cooking to the meals we need today may be a big and difficult change. How do I leave off animal products and still have a healthy diet? How do I go in this direction when no one else in my family seems interested? How do I make the time to learn this new diet? These are legitimate questions but not insurmountable. Just take God on board and see how He leads so amazingly. It's called again "stepping out in faith".

Or you might be at the stage already where God would like for you to be helping others to take those initial steps toward a plant-based diet. We have lots of scientific evidence why people should be doing this. Cancer, heart problems, strokes, diabetes, arthritis, kidney and liver problems, digestive problems, and others are largely related to our poor lifestyles. People tend to eat what tastes good and do what feels good regardless of the consequences. But many people today are ready to make improvements in their lifestyle if they had support and encouragement. Often churches and organizations don't offer this because their goal is in some other direction. I believe this is an important work for Christians, maybe for you. The world is suffering and we can have the answers to make a difference.

Plus, if you have a desire to draw closer to people, to share the love of Jesus, there isn't a better way than to meet their physical needs first. Jesus did this in His ministry regularly: healing people, feeding people, casting out demons, and more. Our lives exemplify the love of God more when we work to meet people's physical needs as well as their spiritual ones. Compassion and sympathy will break down barriers so that Bible truths will be better received later. And some of your greatest experiences will be when you see people gain physical and spiritual victories. You will also experience divine interventions in the process, never to be forgotten; they will keep our faith strong. We will want to share them too, giving us reason to witness. And God gets the glory!

Chapter 4

My Growing Up Years

As much as I would enjoy hearing about your divine interventions, I'm thinking you might be blessed if I would share mine. My experiences may create an idea for you to consider for yourself. Hopefully they will increase your love for God and your faith in Him. God has been so good to me; I can truly say "better than I deserve". So for the most part from here on out, I want to share some of the divine interventions and some of God's leading in my life (now 70 years long).

Let me begin by sharing my background. I was born and raised on a dairy farm in western Pennsylvania. Our income was primarily from the sale of milk, but the farm also included a nice flock of chickens, an orchard, and a large garden. Along with the grains we grew for our horses and cows, we were close to being self-sufficient. Life was fairly hard for our family because we used work horses instead of tractors and milked cows by hand instead of using milking machines. Dad had five sons, which helped a lot in getting the work done. I would say, and neighbors would agree, that we had one of the prettiest farms in the county. Fields of hay and crops were laid out well and pasture fields were clear of weeds and briars.

Though life was hard I knew I was loved, and life was secure and constant because my parents were always home. I did well in school but never was too involved in extra outside activities. We attended Sunday school and church every week. My parents were faithful Presbyterians. Only necessary work was done on Sunday, never any field work. But we always hosted ball games on Sunday afternoon for friends and neighbors: softball, football, or basketball, depending on the season of the year. This was our special recreation for the week. If it was a rainy Sunday afternoon, I was let down.

However, I did enjoy our farm and its work. Growing crops was interesting – seeing plants germinate, blossom, and produce a harvest. Our life depended on doing it well and cooperating with nature. God was always so faithful in our harvests. I also enjoyed the farm animals. Each one was unique with its own personality and we gave each one its own name. I now can relate to Adam in the Garden of Eden as he came to appreciate all the varied animals and was permitted to name them all.

My brothers and I were always faithful in feeding our cows, horses, chickens, cats, and dogs. They were almost like part of the family. Milking the cows was a constant chore, but since it was our main income we seemed to take it in stride. We also sold eggs, vegetables, and fruit through weekly retail deliveries in town. My dad especially enjoyed these weekly excursions because he liked meeting people and making friends. He also enjoyed, as do most gardeners, sharing the fruits of his labors with others.

I, too, began to enjoy these trips to town for the same reasons, plus it was a day that Dad and I could spend together. I remember we would always get a special "treat" to eat. One of our favorites was a glass of buttermilk. I guess we were both real farmers back then. From these weekly sales, Dad was able to buy the necessities we needed for the table for the next week and some "extras" too.

We never had an abundance, but we always had enough. It was "enough", too, because we practiced thriftiness. Little was wasted. Mom was quite a canner of our fruit and vegetables. She was also a good cook who worked hard to feed a husband and five growing boys.

We boys were required to give Mom some help on a regular basis doing dishes and cleaning house. This tradition has been appreciated by my wife through our years of marriage. I'm convinced if the husbands today were a little more helpful with household chores and in raising their children, there would be far fewer marital breakdowns and child delinquency problems. Seeing parents work together has a most positive influence on children.

Growing up as a teen I spent most of my non-school time at home, partly because of the farm workload, and partly because I chose to be home. I didn't date any girls in high school. Not having any sisters, I was very shy around girls and found it hard to connect with them. As a result most of my friends were boys that were in my classes. I had a couple classmates from town that enjoyed coming to our farm to help with the harvesting and other chores. Using horses made the work special for them, and they always enjoyed my mom's dinner.

In high school, teachers encouraged me to take college preparatory classes. So college became my goal for lack of any other goal. I never intended to take over Dad's farm because it was going to require major investment in modernization to stay in business. Many neighboring farms were closing for this reason about this time. And operating costs were rising faster than income.

As I entered my senior year in high school, I still hadn't chosen a field of study or a college to attend. My two oldest brothers, Robert and John, had attended the local Geneva College. My other two brothers, Richard and Carl, had taken up trade employments. I knew I enjoyed the outdoors, but I was having a difficult time deciding on a career choice. Nothing seemed to rise to the top. Most of my classmates were excited about their choices, many looking forward to college life. I kept postponing any decision. The winter of my senior year was upon me and teachers were warning me that it was getting too late to get into most colleges now.

I don't remember praying about my dilemma because I wasn't that deeply religious then. I did feel, however, that God was blessing my life and that things would work out somehow. One day when I was looking over school materials on career choices, I read some about "forest management". It seemed like an interesting possibility. The article described it as more than just achieving the maximum production of timber. It also included managing forests as watersheds for clean water, for recreation, and for fish and wildlife. After a week of talking with my parents and teachers, I applied for entrance at Penn State University and was accepted.

As I look back at this decision, it seemed to be my first divine intervention experience. Though I wasn't an out-going, active Christian, I was open to divine wisdom as to my future. It was going to be a step in faith for this country, home-boy teenager. I was going to be the first of my family to go away to school. As far as I can remember, I had never stayed overnight away from home anytime until then. But I felt this was my call. It was hard for me and my parents when they left me off that next fall. I was now on my own, four hours from home. But God was good to me. I adjusted well and got a job in the cafeteria kitchen to earn some money. The cafeteria staff was a real support to me.

I see this experience as providential because I learned so much about nature those four years. And this knowledge later became my assurance that our world is a result of a wonderful Creator God who sustains it in unbelievably amazing ways. The anatomy and growth of plant life is surprisingly complex and intricate. I thoroughly enjoyed my study at Penn State and thank God for leading me in my learning about His creative work.

Nature is so designed by God to lead us toward Him, even in

its present deteriorating condition. There still remain many awesome evidences of God's beauty, truth, and character in the natural world. Spring renewal of life, autumn colors, sunsets, rainbows, the earth's water cycle, water itself, flowers, insects, animals, and, of course trees, all express a small aspect of our wise and loving Creator.

But Satan can cause a person to be so enamored with these amazing things of nature that the person may spend his life studying nature rather than the God of this nature. I was somewhere in the middle of this paradigm: not leaving God out of it, but still not being drawn to Him. God is so wise and patient. He knows the steps and the direction to take us if we are willing to be led. It may not be straight forward as He would prefer, but if we don't resist, we will be led to Jesus and His salvation.

So God had many more interventions planned for my life that would lead me to a close relationship with Him. This is probably true of most Christians. We advance in limited steps as we give God opportunity to lead us. We often take detours from God's planned travel route, but God will reset His travel plan for us. It's like the resetting of the GPS in our auto after we have taken a wrong road.

Chapter 5

A Turn in My Life

Nearing my graduation date in 1964 with a bachelor's degree in forest management, I was again at a crossroads in my life. Where do I go from here? Some of my classmates were choosing to go on for a master's degree. Well, I wasn't ready for that (and my parents certainly weren't either). This schooling was expensive for our family, even though I had been working through all four years.

Others of my classmates were interviewing for jobs. Somehow this didn't appeal to me yet either. I had just finished 4 hard (for me) years of study and now to accept the first job that was offered me didn't seem the direction I wanted. What could I do? I believe it was at this point that the Lord intervened in my life again. In the spring before graduation I happened to come across a small group of former Peace Corps volunteers who were on campus encouraging enlistments into this new national volunteer program. Somehow this sparked a real interest in me. Of course travel was part of it, but I also believe the Holy Spirit was impressing me to step out in faith and join. He knew that this 2-year service would change the way I viewed the purpose of life: helping those who are less fortunate.

Signing up with the Peace Corps that day still meant that I had to be background-checked and approved by the Peace Corps staff officials. This took a few months during which I sometimes wondered if I had made the right decision. Being a country boy who majored in forestry, I had some doubts that they would find a place for me in a third-world country. My parents would have preferred I had gotten a job. Going to a far off country for two years to try to help others was beyond them. To me it certainly was "thinking out of the box" too, or "stepping out in faith".

In the summer of 1964 I received an invitation from the Peace Corps in Washington, D.C. to go to training in September at the University of Oklahoma in Norman, OK. I was both anxious and excited. The letter stated I was being selected to do forestry work in Peru. I don't think it said much else about what I would be doing. They said training would be two months in Oklahoma and one month in Mexico. It would emphasize cultural and language training, as well as the goals and methods of Peace Corps work. But I found out during training that there was close observation of students by instructors in order to evaluate character, maturity, endurance, courage, etc. These volunteers were to represent the United States.

I remember our group being taken to the Ouachita Mountains in eastern Oklahoma one day to some steep (perpendicular) rock cliffs. Everyone was required to repel down the (maybe 100-foot) rock face and also hold the rope while another repelled down. I had to admit my courage and self-confidence improved that day. We came together more as a group as well. However, as evaluations continued through training, many students were "deselected" and sent home, some of whom I thought had more promise than I did. But God was good to me. I passed the two months on campus, and then I and others were sent to Mexico where we would be mostly on our own for one month. This was to see how well we would adapt to a new culture as well as for improving our Spanish. As many of you know, to learn a language well you have to be in the country where you constantly hear it and are forced to speak it. Other than getting sick occasionally, everything went well. I was now looking forward to Peru.

After the Christmas holidays I was flown to Peru and quickly learned I would be working with the Peruvian Forest Service high in the Andean Mountains. They had a work started that was helping the native Quechua Indian villages to sustain themselves better economically. The program involved starting eucalyptus seedlings in forest service maintained nursery beds, growing them to a foot and a half, and then hauling them in flats to Indian villages that had signed agreements to plant them and care for them. These villages were at more than 12,000 feet in altitude where little tree life existed. No one seemed to know why these mountain areas were barren. But the Peruvian Forest Service (with some outside help, I'm sure) had discovered a couple species of eucalyptus that would thrive there. These were chosen from among other possibilities because they would grow fast and were versatile in their use – for firewood, for housing construction and for sale to mining companies in the area. My part was to assist where I could in the program and give the director more ideas to expand the work.

The area director and I hit off real well. We both liked the reforestation program and we both liked to work. I was his right hand man for my two years in Peru. I ordered seeds of other species of forest trees from the States, which we planted in the nurseries to test their growth rates. I remember spending weeks on a detailed drawing to scale of the nursery and all its different beds, which was sent to forestry headquarters in Lima. Our office seemed to set the pace for others around the country. When the director was transferred to another area, he insisted that I be transferred too. The work did grow and the poor Indian villages were the beneficiaries. But I, too, was a beneficiary because the Lord showed me how to "live life more abundantly" through serving others. Life is not about seeing that I win the race at the end of my life, but is instead about how many I can help win the race with me. It's seeing smiles of appreciation from those less fortunate than I. But I also found that I could learn from them too. The Indians could do craft and handiwork that was amazingly skillful. Their market places in different towns were always a tourist site. I brought home alpaca rugs and wall hangings that were precious.

I also learned from the Peruvians that happiness can be achieved without having much in material goods. They enjoy the simpler life, and have time for friends and family. Many seem to know that true happiness is sharing their lives with others. It was good to know that our forestry work was improving their quality of life and their basic necessities. Yes, I remember coming home telling people that I believe I had gained more than I was able to give. It's always true when we step out in faith. God intervenes to give multiple blessings. God is so good. "His ways are higher than our ways; His thoughts higher than our thoughts." (Isaiah 55:9)

I was privileged to be able to visit Machu Picchu, the historic ruins of the ancient Inca Indian capitol. It is about 50 miles from the city of Cusco, seated on a high mountain. The Incas back then were a powerful, advanced people, governing large parts of Peru, Chile, and Bolivia. Their descendents today are among the poorest in the country. I was glad to be of service to them.

Chapter 6

Discouragement to Joy

Before I left Peru I applied to Duke University for a scholarship toward a 1-year Masters graduate program in forest pathology. I was accepted and so upon arriving back in the States, I went back to school. My goal at this time was to become a forest consultant so that I could help private forest owners with the growth and health of their timberlands. The school year at Duke went by quickly. I did research on a common root disease of Eastern pines called Annosus root rot. I learned a lot about keeping forests healthier which I felt would make me a better consultant. Upon graduation I chose to be interviewed by various private forestry companies for a job because I wanted to get experience before starting my private consultant work. But each company turned me down because of my draft status. My college years and the two years in the Peace Corps had deferred me from getting drafted but had not exempted me. Because of the war in Vietnam, the draft was very active, trying to meet the quota for recruits. Private companies didn't want to hire me, only to then quickly lose me, and have to hold my job open until I returned two years later.

However, the government couldn't refuse me for that reason, so I finally got employment with the U.S. Forest Service in Asheville, NC, working in their Forest Insect and Disease Branch.

Sure enough, several months after getting hired I received my draft notice to report to Fort Dix, NJ for Army training. I was quite upset. I was now 6 months from turning 26 which would put me out of reach of the draft. I had no positive feelings toward the Vietnam War and less desire still to go there. I was pretty much a pacifist at heart. One way around this problem was to enlist and get a work more to my liking. So I enlisted (for 3 years) asking for the Corps of Engineers and to become an officer. They agreed but I still would have to go to basic training and advanced infantry training (AIT), before I could go to Officers Candidate School (OCS) at Fort Benning, GA. So off I went to Fort Dix, NJ. where I completed basic training in the cold of winter and then the AIT right after. Half way through OCS in the summer of 1968 the need for infantry officers was so great that the call came down from Washington that all candidates (unless they had direct orders otherwise) were going to be assigned to the infantry. My orders apparently weren't "direct", so I was heading for Vietnam as an infantry officer.

This, to me, was worse than going over as an enlisted man. I would be leading others into battle for a war I didn't support. So I dropped out of OCS. This meant I was now back to being an infantry enlisted man with 2 years of service. My orders were to go to Vietnam in a few weeks as a private. I thought about the idea of going to Canada to escape it all. But that is when the Lord stepped into my life in a marked manner again. I felt a very strong impression (nothing audible) that if I went on to Vietnam, God would see that I wouldn't have to shoot at anyone and I wouldn't get shot at. This was some promise! I still was not at this time a strong Christian but I believed this must be from God. I decided to believe this impression and accept my orders to go to Vietnam.

My flight there was a long one, giving me a lot of time to wonder how this was all going to work out. Upon arrival in Vietnam I was assigned to a supportive unit attached to the 173rd Airborne Brigade in the central highlands. I knew there was a lot of action there. When I arrived at my unit, I felt led to go to the personnel management office of the brigade headquarters. I met a pleasant Black warrant officer in charge of the office. I introduced myself and told him about my college and Peace Corps background and my time in the Army thus far. I then suggested to him that I thought I might be of more value to them in some way other than carrying a rifle. Praise the Lord, he said that may be true. He asked if I would like to work in his office; he would give me a 30-day trial. I learned well those 30 days and took on responsibility. A lot of it was record keeping on troop levels, troop losses and injuries, and needed replacements. After 30 days he agreed to keep me on his staff. I was so thankful for God's providence.

It was the requirement of all enlisted men at the headquarters area to do night guard duty a couple times a week on the perimeter encircling the headquarters. Therefore over the 52 weeks I was in Vietnam, I must have been on night perimeter duty 90 times. A lot of action took place at these guard posts, but never did it happen in my section when I was on duty. Amazing! God is faithful. I served under two different officers in my work that year and they both gave me a week of R&R (rest and recuperation). So I enjoyed short vacations to nearby Singapore and to Sydney. That was one more R&R than most soldiers got, but our office was the one that cut the orders for R&R. Another blessing! But there was yet another one. After my year was up and I returned to the States at Fort Lewis in Washington, it was determined that I had less than 90 days until my 2 years were up. I was told that this was too short a time for a reassignment and that they would discharge me then and there. I didn't argue.

There were two close friends I had in the 173rd that came back the same time I did and were released for the same reason. So we decided to rent a car together and enjoy a trip across the U.S.A. We went down along the Pacific coast to San Francisco (enjoyed a day of horse racing), and then on to Las Vegas (spent a couple dollars) and to the Grand Canyon. It was so great to be free again. God is so good! We went from Arizona on to Kentucky where the one friend lived, then on to Pennsylvania where I lived. The other friend returned the car in Boston where he lived. God planned it out well. My parents were ever so glad to see me again. My mom had been such a faithful letter writer and an encourager while I was in Vietnam. Actually she had been my encourager ever since I had gone off to college over 9 years before. I know she and Dad had prayed a lot during those years too. More than I had! But God "was still working on me".

This whole military experience was a good example of how God enables us to go through a difficulty rather than taking us around it. He could have had my name never come up until I was past 26 years old. But instead, He helped me go right through the difficulty, not even letting me join the Corps of Engineers. Otherwise, I would have missed out on a lot of faith-building experiences that mean a lot to me today. Building faith in God is the core of life. Our life, short or longer, is primarily to determine our choice for eternity, as well as helping others to make that choice. Satan steals that focus from us by having us put our attention on our life here: work, amusements, hobbies, sports, music, family, church, and more. I've used examples that aren't bad, but these can be taken to the extreme so that our focus isn't on our Saviour and a growing faith in Him. When Jesus comes again, He will be looking for those having faith in Him. (Luke 18:8)

Chapter 7

My Introduction to Adventists

After the military experience I returned to the job at the U.S. Forest Service in Asheville, NC. My first item of business was to find housing. I searched the want-ads for an apartment outside of town, private, and not too expensive. I wasn't actively asking the Lord to lead in my choice, but I'm so thankful that He is anxious to lead if we don't resist. I looked at several possibilities but wasn't completely satisfied. Then I looked at a garage apartment in Arden, south of Asheville. It had a beautiful setting, with pretty azaleas and Rhododendrons, and was private and affordable. I liked the older couple, Richard and Rena Hollar, from the start. And wouldn't you know, I found out very soon that they were Seventh-day Adventists, the first I had ever met. They were so friendly and hospitable. This was to be another major divine intervention in my life as I became acquainted with this couple and their church denomination.

For now, I was ready to go back to work. And for awhile it was comfortable to be in a good-paying, secure position, doing outdoor work for the most part. The other employees were friendly and encouraging. On weekends the men liked to go golfing together. I had never gotten into this sport, but when the office manager invited me to join them and he said he had an older set of golf clubs to give me, I gladly said "sure". I caught on fairly well and enjoyed the opportunity to get to know everyone better. I could also join in on the golf stories during coffee breaks on Monday mornings. I also enjoyed the travel involved in my work. We went by car or plane all over the Southeast to evaluate forest disease problems and make necessary recommendations. Back then (1970) we were also just getting involved in how industrial pollution was affecting our forests. I had particular interest in this new work. So, work started out well.

As the weeks went by, my friendship with the Hollars grew. They would continually invite me to have lunch with them. Being single and not a cook, I accepted fairly often. I quickly found out they were vegetarian. Though food was a little different, it still tasted quite good. They had no children but they treated me as if I were one. I would do outside chores occasionally for them. A couple times they asked if I would drive for them on a day trip somewhere. And they always shared literature with me which I didn't always read. They also invited me to church often (on Saturdays?). I always seemed to have other things planned on that day (like golfing). But I admit they made me feel loved and appreciated. This is an important first step in reaching someone for Jesus. They spoke freely of Jesus and this was a new experience for me. My parents and other Christians I knew in the past seldom spoke of Jesus in a personal way on a daily basis.

The Christmas Season soon came around that year and our office was planning its annual office party. Everyone was expected to take their spouse or a date. Well, I hadn't yet met any young ladies. About this same time the Hollar's niece (Betty) came to

My Introduction to Adventists // 35

visit them for a few days. Betty was married and had her 2-month old daughter with her. I learned that she was going through some difficult bumps in her marriage. Her husband was in the Navy and it seemed that he was getting deeply involved in drugs. Mrs. Hollar was very troubled about this relationship. She had helped to raise Betty, keeping her months at a time when she was younger, and she felt toward Betty like a mother would.

When Mrs. Hollar found out that I needed a date for the Christmas party she encouraged Betty to go with me. Betty was surprised her Christian aunt would make such a suggestion. She responded with, "I'm a married woman!" Well, needless to say, she didn't go with me. But Mrs. Hollar wasn't ready to give up on getting the two of us together, at least in a friendship.

She later asked me to write Betty and encourage her during the difficult circumstances of being a single parent, once Betty had decided to separate from her husband. I might not have agreed to do this except for the fact that this girl was pretty attractive and, to be the Hollar's favorite niece, probably a nice wholesome lady. So, letter writing began between the two of us.

Betty always responded nicely and in good time, telling me about her life. She soon got a divorce, and when the 4th of July came around with some vacation time, I volunteered to come visit her. She now lived in Albuquerque, NM, of all places. When I arrived she appeared very reserved, not like her letters. We had a cordial couple days together, but I left feeling this was the end. She did write later, maybe on her aunt's request, that it was probably still too close to her divorce to be able to develop another relationship. I didn't write after that. Mrs. Hollar didn't continue pursuing it either. But the Lord still had other plans down the road.

As my forestry work continued for the next several months, it became more routine. And one thing my life wasn't used to was routine. I began thinking about the time when work was the most satisfying, and it led me back to when I was in the Peace Corps. What could I do here in the States that would be similar. I learned somehow about public-funded community action agencies that exist around the country. Like the Peace Corps, their goal is to help people help themselves. I also learned there were some in western NC. I began checking for openings for work in these agencies. Soon I found an opening for a county supervisor position in Transylvania County for Western Carolina Community Action, Inc. (WCCA). This position included supervising several local community workers as well as 6 to10 VISTA (Volunteers In Service To America) volunteers. VISTA was like an in-country Peace Corps. WCCA also operated various programs such as Head Start which benefit poor families. It sounded very attractive to me. But should I leave my bread-and-butter career? Let all my forestry education go? My forestry workmates thought it would be crazy to do this. My newer job would pay so much less. My family thought, too, I was making a big mistake, but my mom and dad seemed to have more understanding.

 I thought hard about it but didn't directly ask God. I still hadn't come to that point yet. But I did think that enjoying my work was more important than making good money. I had come to the point where I told folks that "I enjoyed working with people more than with trees". So, at last, I figured that if I got the job it must be meant for me. Soon I went to the WCCA office in Hendersonville, NC (the main office of the 2-county agency) to turn in my application and have an interview. I met with a tall, somewhat disabled Black man who seemed to be one of the most compassionate men I had ever met. We talked about my background and his agency's work. It was a lot like the Peace Corps, so he and I hit off very well. I soon heard from him that I was hired.

 This decision led me another step closer to finding my Saviour. I certainly wasn't aware of it but the Lord was patiently guiding me. I here had found a work that was keeping my heart tender toward

Him until the right people came together to lead me to accepting Jesus. I wasn't resisting His leading but I wasn't yet searching for Him either. This reminds me of a favorite statement that says if we do not resist the Holy Spirit, we will be saved. What a precious God we serve. When I look back at the timing of everything for this new work, it was providential. I was meant to be living in Brevard in Transylvania County for the next few years of my life.

Chapter 8

God's Hand Over Me

I really enjoyed my new work with Western Carolina Community Action. The down side of it, however, was that I had to leave my nice apartment in Arden with the Hollars. We were all sad that I had to leave, but they seemed to understand my reasons, for it was best that I live in the county where I would be working. And Arden is 25 miles from Brevard, too far to commute in my view. Transylvania County lives up to its name, having forests from border to border. So if I wasn't going to be working in forestry, I could at least live near forests.

I was again looking for an apartment. I found a basement apartment near the edge of town on a quiet street. It supplied the minimum needs nicely and it was what I could afford. The owner was an elderly lady who was approaching the point where she couldn't stay by herself. Her son regularly checked on her and things had been going well. The son was a professor at the Brevard College and much involved with their Music Center, a well-respected center for quality music instruction and concerts. This is what put Brevard on the map, so to speak. Quality music was not a high priority of mine at that time, but the college still was a nice influence on the town. My priority now was getting acquainted with my new work and its people.

I was given a better welcome than I really deserved because their previous county supervisor had done such a poor job that they assumed that I had to be better than him. Plus they had never met anyone who had been in the Peace Corps. The local community workers were doing a good job and were glad to have me show a sincere interest in their work. The most recent VISTA group had come to a close (they serve for a year) and the next group was beginning training in Atlanta, GA. My first work was to quickly write a proposal for more VISTA volunteers and explain what work we had for them. This required some hasty research, a lot of it gained by talking to the staff that had been on board for some time. The one I relied on most was my secretary, Rachel. Her knowledge and insights were superior. She helped me get the information, and my college experience helped me get it into the right format. Rachel and I worked well together for the several years I was there. She was knowledgeable and dependable. This is in contrast to many people who get into community action work who are idealistic but aren't too pragmatic.

The proposal I sent to Atlanta was approved. I then had to go there to meet the candidates and help decide who should come back to Transylvania County. Most, but not all VISTA volunteers, were still in college (and taking a break) or had just graduated. A few were in their mid-life years, which was fine too. All were usually from upper middle-income families and the more urban societies. So, you can guess where some of my effort was focused: getting them adjusted to rural poor communities. This is when I was thankful for being raised in a rural, lower income home.

I had weekly meetings with our VISTA volunteers to discuss questions, ideas, and challenges they faced. The local community workers met with us too, which made for some good interchange.

I also would meet with everyone regularly in their distinctive work areas. We made progress together and the head office in Hendersonville seemed satisfied that work had gained some momentum and that our office raised no further crises.

Work was taking most of my energies. Working with people, even nice people, can be draining. I didn't take time to seek out lady friends. I still had this country bashfulness around the opposite sex. One community worker from the other county, Henderson County, introduced me to her daughter who was a single banker in Toronto. She was an urbanite, of course, but we still seemed to enjoy each other's company. However, this was only on her vacations to visit her family. We wrote some but that only takes one so far in a relationship. I wondered, though, if this was the best I could expect.

About this time I also was trying to play out in my mind where I wanted to stand on my religious life. I had kept putting God on the back burner, even though I could see how He was stepping into my life at different times. I hadn't been much of a church attender since I had left Penn State. This was 7 years now. I felt I needed to do a search on churches. I knew I didn't want any "hell fire and brimstone" church, and I didn't want a church with "ritual services" for worship. I did want one that seemed to care for and serve the community. Even though the Hollars had demonstrated true Christianity, it somehow never entered my mind to include the Seventh-day Adventist Church in my search, maybe because they went on the wrong day to fit my life schedule.

After some study and some visits, I decided to try the Unitarian Church. Religious folks probably thought I was going in the wrong direction. But the Unitarian Church in Asheville was a little different than the one, say, in Boston. They used the Bible as part of their scripture reading, along with well-known philosophers, and included principles from the Bible in their sermons. I rather liked the church's interest in making the world better, and not dwelling on sin, doom, and gloom.

In this church you could take what you wanted and leave behind what you didn't want. I was into forming my own religious thinking and this seemed to fit me fine. The pastor was older, and maybe more conservative, than most Unitarian pastors. Members were middle-class and friendly, but not the type that insisted that I get involved in some part of their church work. I could enjoy the service, the positive message, and some hand shakes and then be able to go home.

But this religious lethargy wasn't to last too many months. Out of the blue one day, I received a letter from Betty at my office. She was working in Chicago, having come from California a few months before that. The gist of the letter was about what I was doing, was I still single, and would I have any interest in getting reacquainted. Well, in my current social status, I certainly had room for one more. She mentioned then, or shortly thereafter, that she had become a Seventh-day Adventist. And she said she would be willing to move to Arden, to be near her aunt and uncle, and this would also make it easier for us to get acquainted. If things didn't work out for us, she said she would still enjoy living near the Hollars. So I agreed she should make the move. I wasn't sure how her being an Adventist was going to play out in our relationship.

It wasn't long before she did move. She didn't want to spend a cold winter in Chicago. I went to see her a few days later. She looked much the same but her daughter, Renée, was now 2 years old. I don't remember feeling "wowed" at seeing her. I was single and she was a mother, although a pretty one. I had always pictured myself marrying a single girl and then enjoying a few years together before having children. This didn't fit the picture, but we at least could be friends. She told me how she had attended some evangelistic meetings in California held by E.E. Cleveland and, at the close, she had given her heart to Jesus and decided to join the Adventist Church. I don't remember how she looked when I told her I was attending the Unitarian Church. But she was probably somewhat dismayed. Our religions could be considered at opposite poles.

Another thing I learned quickly was that Betty was now a vegetarian, like her aunt and uncle. When we later had a lunch together at her home, I actually enjoyed it; it reminded me of lunches I used to enjoy with the Hollars. I remember early on, too, that she didn't like coffee or tobacco. Both were prevalent in my circles. I had even picked up a little smoking to be more sociable. I would use Listerine mouth wash before visiting Betty, and I would wonder how she could still smell smoke on me. Now I can easily understand. But she was kind and patient with me, and appreciated the type of work I was doing.

She was soon employed close to her home. A friend of the Hollars owned a health food store in Asheville, and he hired Betty as a clerk. Betty enjoyed meeting people and encouraging and helping them toward better health. She was still a new Adventist and had that "first love" to serve the Lord. (It is a continued challenge, as Christians, to keep that enthusiastic and vibrant first love experience for Jesus. We need to keep stepping forward in faith, growing in the Lord.) Betty took her daughter, Renée, to a nearby daycare during her work hours. At 2 years old, Renée was well able to express her desires already. She had quickly acquired the nickname "bulldozer" at the daycare. She could be a handful at home too.

As different as Betty and I seemed to be, we still enjoyed each other's company, especially when the topic wasn't religion. We both had rural, lower middle-income backgrounds, enjoyed the outdoors, and the simpler life. It wasn't long until she was inviting me to church, like a good Christian would. I often had other plans or commitments, but occasionally I would agree to go. I would think that this wasn't too different than going to a Presbyterian or Methodist church. If only they would meet on Sundays, it would be easier and fewer "eyebrows raised". However, I noticed that the Asheville area of NC sure had a lot of people who seemed to fit the Sabbath into their schedule all right. I hadn't yet agreed to do any Bible study on the subject, although I did understand that the 4th commandment of the 10 clearly said to keep the 7th day holy.

The year went by quickly for the first VISTA group I supervised. They were good compassionate people who tried their best to work with the local folks to improve their lot in life. One fellow, Lew, from western New York, and I have stayed in touch and have made occasional visits through the years. He is now a retired teacher, has a nice family, and loves the Lord.

At the end of this first year, the group was replaced by a second group of VISTAS soon after. This group included a couple of cute college-aged girls. They were assigned to a lower-income area on the edge of town. I didn't plan it that way at the beginning, but it resulted in my being able to have more contact with them than some of the other volunteers. This caused a little turmoil in my mind and a bump in the road with my relationship with Betty.

These girls were single with no ties to guys that I knew of, and appreciated my friendship and "expertise" in helping them in their community work. My emotional thoughts wanted to see where this road might lead. But I felt I needed to keep it on a business level; it would otherwise negatively affect the whole county program. Betty met the girls a couple times and she knew she had competition. I remember one time the two girls needed a ride to Asheville and they asked me to take them. This made Betty quite jealous. It wasn't too long after (around Valentine's Day, 1972) that Betty wanted to discuss our future. She said she didn't want to be just friends. If we didn't go to the next level of courtship, she said she would feel better not dating anymore. I was caught a little off guard. I guess I hadn't been giving our relationship enough thought, with the Canadian girl and these VISTA volunteers befriending me too.

The Lord intervened that very evening. He had me to understand clearly and quickly that life with these other girls would possibly be more fun for awhile, but the road on ahead was most likely in a worldly direction. Christianity wasn't an obvious influence in their lives, as it was with Betty and her daughter Renée. Although I hadn't turned my life over to Jesus yet, I had respect for Betty's commitment to her Lord and to raising her daughter for Him. I knew she would be a more positive influence on me and a better companion for me. I felt a strong urge to make that life-changing decision that evening, before I lost it. So I asked her to marry me, and she just as quickly said "yes". Our love had been silently growing over the past several months, but that evening we felt we had made a good decision. So much so that we decided right then to get married the first Sunday of May, when spring would be bursting. I look back at how amazing the Lord led in my thoughts concerning this major decision in my life. In the area of love and marriage we need to seek God's wisdom to discern the difference between love and infatuation. Love has a reasonable basis to it, while infatuation is mere fantasy.

Now it is commonly understood and accepted that Seventh-day Adventist members should not marry a non-member, or for sure a non-Christian. So this issue quickly came up when church members learned that she was engaged to a man attending a Unitarian Church. Some strongly told her she was making a mistake (and at times during the next 2 years she would have agreed). But now she would respond that they didn't even know me, so how could they pass judgment.

When my Easter vacation came around, I asked Betty (and Renée) to go with me to visit my family. This would be her first opportunity to do so. My parents liked Betty and Renée from the start and could see we could be a good mutual support for each other. At 29 it was time for me to settle down, and Betty and Renée needed a "good" man in their life. My parents couldn't foresee what problems our religious differences might cause. But an evening or two later, while visiting my younger brother and his wife, our discussions disclosed how wide apart Betty and I stood theologically. Betty was quite alarmed and began thinking she was making a mistake. She decided to end our engagement that night.

The next day was Easter. In the morning, on hearing this news, my parents were so disheartened they couldn't even go to church. But Betty stood her ground, even when my brother John, a Presbyterian pastor, came by in the afternoon to try to resolve the issue. So the following morning, we headed back to North Carolina quite a bit more subdued. I could only think that if she was this "extreme" about her religion, it might well be best to call off the engagement.

During the next few weeks we continued to visit. She attended the Unitarian Church with me a few Sundays but this didn't help our relationship. So I would more often agree to go with her to the Adventist Church. I guess Betty began to see more hope in our future and how I could be a good father for Renée. I helped her financially once in a tight spot and she appreciated my concern and support for her. We soon put the May 7 wedding date back on the calendar. I thought it had been good to go through some rough spots before we got married.

Betty didn't want to get married in a Unitarian Church and the Adventist pastor felt he couldn't marry us because of our religious differences, so we agreed on a friend of mine (through work), who was a Presbyterian pastor. The night before we were to get married, Betty's ex-husband showed up somewhat high on drugs and said if we carried through on the wedding, he was going to shoot me. So my brother, John, and I reported it to the police. They told me they really couldn't arrest him until he actually did something. Well that was comforting! Betty was concerned too. The next morning I drove to the outdoor chapel (Pretty Place, SC) where we were to get married, not knowing for sure if Betty would choose to be there or not. Thankfully she did and her ex-husband did not.

It was a perfect wedding. The day was cool but sunny. From the chapel the view extended far and down into South Carolina. Escorted by her uncle, she looked her prettiest coming down the aisle in her light blue dress. I felt like the most blessed man on earth. And God had been the Guide. Pastor McPhail did the service nicely. My family was all there to enjoy it with us. Betty's mom was able to be there and she kept Renée while we went to Florida for our honeymoon. I felt (and I was) in a brand new world, the world of married life. It is meant to be different than single life, especially when marrying into fatherhood too. One has a companion whose needs and concerns are as important as your own. Spouses learn to be unselfish and to share their life (joys and sorrows) with this special person. In marriage there is to be mutual support and cooperation. And the work that the couple can do for the Lord is greater than what they could have done living separately. So we can see why marriage is the core of society and of God's church. How well marriage fares is how well society and the church will fare.

Chapter 9

Accepting Jesus As My Saviour

Work, on our return from Florida, continued to go well. We rented a home outside of town. There was room for Renée and her new little dog, Boy. I had my first garden since I had left home for college. It did well. The Lord was good to us. I continued attending church with her; now we went to a smaller church near Brevard. She had decided not to go to the Unitarian Church anymore, and so I decided to stop too. And since I felt the family ought to attend church together, I attended most every Sabbath with Betty and Renée. I had gotten to like the people at this country church. They treated me like a member though I had no intentions at this time to become one.

I remember one Sabbath I had been asked to give the mission story for Sabbath School the following week. As I read the story ahead of time, I realized I had visited the very spot where the story took place when I was in the Peace Corps in Peru. The place was the floating reed islands on Lake Titicaca. There is an Adventist school for the families living out there. But it is also a tourist attraction because these islands are made only of reeds that have built up over centuries of time. Boats will take visitors out to see these unique islands. When I went I didn't realize it was an Adventist work going on there, so the story was quite interesting to me.

Through the following months I began to appreciate the world-wide work of the Seventh-day Adventist Church. Besides missionary and evangelistic work, there was much "community action" work that they did, helping people to help themselves through better education, economic aid, and disaster relief. They seemed to put their Christian principles into action to a higher degree than any religion I knew. One way they do so much is that every faithful member not only tithes his 10% to the denomination for spreading the gospel, but he also gives 5-10% or more to other work of the church and for upkeep of their own church building. And God blesses these individuals and their generosity. Also, for the economic aid and disaster relief work in third world countries, the Adventists receive much outside money to assist in these aid programs. They have a reputation of using donated monies for only the designated purpose, and not for organizational costs.

It wasn't long again until the year was up for our second VISTA group. Similar to the Peace Corps volunteers, these volunteers sometimes ended their tour with some disillusion with what they accomplished compared to what they had hoped to accomplish. But I felt this group had done well. The biggest tangible accomplishment was starting up a nice consignment store in town specializing in arts and crafts of local citizens. The man who worked on this project with us had contacts in New York City and elsewhere who were glad to take orders for these southern mountain crafts. Quilts especially went well. I don't remember how I got in touch with him. He wasn't a local man. This seemed to be another leading of God.

As is common with government money, our funds for VISTA

came to an end. And the federal funds through the Office of Economic Opportunity also were cut back. This left a severe down-sizing in our office. Some of the current work would certainly continue, but no innovative new work could be funded. With fewer workers and less work to oversee, I felt stymied. I needed a new work. So I resigned from my position. That's when my entrepreneurship kicked in and this led into my next divine intervention experience.

My new thought was to open an attractive produce stand along the 4-lane highway coming into town from Asheville. I would buy fresh produce in bulk from local gardeners and resale it. I would also buy produce from a large warehouse in Greenville, SC to add to my stock. This would include produce grown further south and out of the region. I bought an older pick-up truck to make these trips and borrowed a little money to have a produce stand built. I started in early spring selling mostly produce from the Greenville warehouse, but soon I was buying produce from local people. By summer business was going fairly well.

It was then that a lay evangelist, Fred, from our local Adventist church wanted to do a series of public meetings in Brevard using a large outdoor tent. He searched everywhere for a site to set up his tent, but no place seemed suitable or he couldn't get permission if it was. So he came to me asking if he could use the property near my produce stand to set up his tent. I told him "no thanks" and said it would probably hurt my business and interfere with visibility. He came back in a few days saying he still hadn't found a place. Would I agree? I told him "Sorry!" In a few more days he returned again, saying that it was time to get on with his meetings. Would I please say "yes"?

Well, I began feeling bad for him. He really was a friend at the church and I had studied a little with him on the Daniel prophecies. So I reluctantly said "OK", though I felt I wouldn't be attending them.

His meetings started pretty quickly. Betty was assuming I would attend all of them since they were on my rented property, and hoping I would make a firm decision for Jesus. She was having times of frustration with my reluctance to get serious with the Lord. But her "pressuring" me didn't help either. So as the meetings started I didn't attend many nights. This added to her frustration and our communication difficulties. When I had nothing else to do, I would attend occasionally. She didn't know it, but what I did hear made an impression on me. For sometime now I agreed with the teachings of the church, but my resistance was admitting that I needed a Saviour. I had gained a self-confidence that my "good life" was pleasing to God and any "shortages" I may have at life's end, God would justly take care of. I was trying to combine the best of the Unitarian and Adventist beliefs. But as I began to see the true holiness of God, I, like Isaiah, could see my "unholiness". I was far from "good".

Near the end of Fred's meetings I was there when he gave a strong sermon asking for a commitment to accept the truths he had been sharing from the Bible. He reminded us how Jesus and His Word must be the firm foundation for our life. Without that we are like the house built on the sand that so easily falls in the storm. When Fred called for those to come forward who wanted to follow Jesus and His truth, I was the first one to respond and go forward. Betty was so caught off guard that she later asked me what my going up meant to me. When I told her I was accepting Jesus as my Saviour and would be joining the Adventist Church, she cried with joy. I, too, was happy, but I was already wondering where life with Jesus was going to lead me. I knew it would be different from now on.

Chapter 10

A Big Step

I continued having a busy summer with produce, making trips early in the morning to Greenville to restock my stand. I had a good number of local people bringing in fruit and vegetables and I enjoyed getting to know them. I don't remember that I boldly talked about my decision to follow Jesus, but I enjoyed sharing it when the topic came up. Life seemed more complete; Jesus says it becomes more abundant. But Satan likes to test your resolve in following Jesus all the way, especially at the beginning. He wants to trip you up before you get too solid in your new life direction.

As the fall season progressed I had less local produce to offer, but I still did well with the outside produce I brought in. However, as the weather got cooler fewer people wanted to stop at an open stand. I specialized in pumpkins for awhile, then finally Christmas trees. I knew by then I didn't have enough money saved to bide me over the winter until I could reopen in the spring. So I gave up on this idea of produce to see if I could get a regular 40-hour per week work. I look back at that one season with the produce stand as God positioning me for hearing His Word and making a firm decision to follow Him. It seemed uncanny that Fred couldn't find anywhere to put up his tent except on my property. A divine intervention! More amazing ones were to come as I began to step out in faith.

I sent out resumes to a few local schools and colleges for possible teaching positions. No results! Other interviews weren't productive either. With money getting tighter, I took a school bus driving job, did some window washing work for different home owners, and other odd jobs. The Lord provided what we needed. By this time, we were living in a home (for about a year now) that we had purchased near the old hospital in town and were making payments. Renée, now 4, enjoyed the neighborhood enough to just walk outside and go visit people on her own. Betty would have to call the neighbors to see which one she was visiting today and tell her it was time to come home.

But since I wasn't finding work, we began wondering where the Lord wanted us to go. About this time we heard of an Adventist in Wytheville, VA, Dr. Malin, who wanted help to reopen an Adventist academy there. I thought maybe I could teach there. He was glad to have us come and he offered me work on his dairy farm until it reopened. So, sorry as we were to leave Brevard, we headed to Virginia. We sold our house a few months after our move. The dairy farm work turned out to be milking cows morning and evening. It wasn't the most exciting work, but I needed work and hopefully the academy would be opening soon.

We first moved into an apartment, but soon Dr. Malin offered us a house that he owned where we could live without rent. The best way to get to the house was across a swinging bridge and up a path. Otherwise one had to take a long dirt road to come in from the back. The house had water but no bathrooms. There was only a nice path to a "nice" outhouse. Betty was pregnant now and wasn't too excited about taking that little path so often, or, for that matter, the big path across the swinging bridge. Sometimes Betty and Renée would come home after dark and Renée insisted that Betty carry her across the swinging bridge. Betty would tell her: "If I lose this baby...." We were all learning to persevere.

We did enjoy the church in Wytheville. It was a larger church than Brevard and offered more for the family. We were invited to help with Sabbath afternoon services in a nearby community. This made a full day but we enjoyed helping. We made friends with a literature evangelist leader, Bob, who also attended our church. Literature evangelism is working as an evangelist through the selling of Christian literature in people's homes. As the children and adult books are shown to people, this provides an opportunity for the salesman to encourage people to read the Bible and follow Jesus. It's a work of faith because the income is solely a commission on the sales made. Many enjoy the work for this reason. Stepping out in faith for the Lord, they experience many divine interventions and are given many wonderful opportunities to spiritually touch people's lives. They learn the power of prayer for themselves and the families they meet.

Bob somehow thought I could be a literature evangelist (LE). He asked me to join in the work so often that Betty thought I could do it too. I guess she thought it would be a lot better than the smelly farm work. (Since she was experiencing "morning sickness", she would have me undress outside when I came home from work.) But being new in the church, my faith didn't stretch far. I would tell Bob that I wasn't cut out for sales work. He would say "that's good; that's where the Lord wants you, so He can do the work for you". But I would shake my head and say "no thanks". One Sabbath Bob was guest speaker at Wytheville. And of course he spoke about being active in the Lord's service. I probably squirmed in my seat. Betty had previously arranged for him and his family to come home for lunch after church.

So there I was, a captive audience. I had promised him the previous week that I would pray about it, and I had. And it seemed that the Lord was now working on Bob's side. I also knew by now that the academy was not going to take off, and that milking cows wasn't in my future. So, when Bob asked me one more time, I finally consented to take my step in faith. He gave me a written canvass to memorize to help get me started. I was never one who could memorize anything very well, so this was a challenge from the start. But Bob was encouraging and patient with me. It would take a special person to train this boy into Christian salesmanship, and Bob was the one that God had chosen.

While I was memorizing the various canvasses, I went out with him each day to observe how he met people, canvassed them, shared Jesus, closed the sale, and had prayer with the family. He would leave the home as a true friend. His work was truly evangelistic. As his trainee, any sales he made would go on record as my sale. We were mostly working in Roanoke, VA which was to be my future work area. Actually "work area" meant where you were permitted to advertise for leads. Other LEs also had their assigned advertising area. Leads were obtained through the placement of sample books containing lead cards in public waiting rooms such as doctor's offices and hospitals. People could take the attached card and send it in for more information. The Bible Stories by Arthur Maxwell was a favorite for families, so we used sample copies of this a lot. But LEs don't depend only on leads; they also knock on other doors too, with good success.

After a full week of going out with Bob, he asked me to try going out on my own near my home the following Sunday (without a lead card). I met a family down the road, was invited in, and sold a complete Bible Story set with an adult book. I was so excited I could hardly write up the order. And I prayed with them from a thankful heart. I called Bob when I got home and he seemed surprised ("You did?") as well as pleased. I guess Betty was too. But this was the beginning of four years of faith-building experiences. We were truly dependent on the Lord. Stepping out in faith will bring divine interventions every time.

We soon moved to Roanoke, to an apartment area on the north side. This wasn't our first choice, but it was lower rent and convenient for Betty to meet doctor appointments. Betty was soon to deliver our first child. Pregnant women and new babies were words never in my vocabulary before. Every week was a new experience. Betty had gained a lot of weight, some in her face too, and she looked prettier than ever. Her sister thought so too. But I told her I couldn't afford to keep her that way. Soon little Nelson Shaun came into the world. That's when my world changed some more. They take so much time, and they cry so much (and at night). Kidding Betty, I asked her if she was sure she had brought the right one home. But I wouldn't have traded him. Renée was in "heaven", getting to be a little mother a lot of the time.

My work was going well for a beginner. The Lord was providing for our needs, but not much extra though. My LE leader advised me to always put in my time (40 hours) and the Lord would bless. I was always home at night, but the best hours to make visits were in the afternoon and evening. Some calls took me 2-3 hours away from home. But I would spend the whole day in that area. Betty and Renée would always pray for my travel safety and my visits. Most people were so friendly, and even if they couldn't buy anything, I would leave a free paperback and a Bible correspondence course invitation card.

Before our year lease was up at the apartment, Betty was feeling the need to leave the not-so-good environment there. The noise was loud and Renée's friends weren't a good influence on her. The apartment manager said we could leave if they found someone to move into it. So we put in our 30-day notice and told her to start looking and we would have another place by the time she found someone. Well, she found someone fairly quickly. However, as we checked advertisements, made calls and visits, we came up with nothing day after day. After 15 days the manager asked when we would be moving out. We told her we didn't know where yet, but we would be out on time. After another week this exchange was repeated. Finally Betty saw an ad for a brick home for rent in Wirtz, VA, over 15 miles south of Roanoke. I said that was too far. But she insisted that we should look at it and then decide. We all went out and we decided that this was where the Lord had chosen. It had some older apple trees, a place for a garden, and space for Renée to play.

However, the owners had told the realtor handling the home that families with children were not to be considered. The realtor, though, had come to appreciate our little family and told the owners he thought we would be safe renters. They agreed he should use his own judgment in the matter. One evening before I came home, he stopped by for a visit. Betty was reading a Bible Story when he came to the door. She invited him in but told him she wanted to finish worship with the children first and asked him to join them. So he quietly sat and listened until Betty was finished. At this point, he kindly told her the house was ours and gave her the keys, all without even receiving any money! He had seen enough to convince him we would be good renters. So, we moved out of the apartment just in time, 1 or 2 days before the end of the month. Isn't God good? Someone has said that "God is seldom early, but never late". He knows how to intervene in our lives at just the right time to manifest He is in control of our lives.

God made these interventions regularly during my work time too. I often came home at night with one or more inspirational experiences to tell Betty. I still remember a favorite experience that took place not far from our Wirtz home. We usually lived from pay check to pay check, and we often knew what I needed to sell to meet the following week's bills. This particular week was one of those. It would have to be a fairly good week. I worked faithfully that week, had some wonderful visits, but no larger sales. I would come home disappointed. On my last work day of the week I had high hopes that this was to be a good day. I had plenty of presentations during the day but no sales. I was now without leads and it was getting dark. I don't prefer to knock on cold doors at night. I wasn't far from home when I stopped to pray. I told the Lord that I couldn't go home yet. Where did he want me to go?

Almost immediately I was impressed to go to a German Baptist home a few miles away. I had been there before some months earlier, but somehow the time wasn't right for them to buy. So, I drove to their home, was kindly invited in, and made the presentation before the whole family. I showed them the Bible Story set, the large adult set, and the family Bible. They decided to buy everything and pay cash. A cash sale was a higher commission than one financed. So my week was complete! Again, I prayed for the family and that their use of this purchase would be to God's glory. But I also had sincere prayers of thanks on the way home for His perfect leading. This, to me, was another personal divine intervention.

Every literature evangelist hopes to see some positive spiritual results form his work as he carries it out day by day. I had that privilege one day working in Roanoke. The person I wanted to see that day wasn't home, so, as LEs often do, I began knocking on a few doors nearby to see if the Lord had someone else for me to see in the area. Very soon I rang the door bell of a home in which a lady inside called for me to come in. I slowly entered the door. The house was dark and I tried to see where the voice came from. As my eyes adjusted to the darkness, I saw a lady sitting on the couch. I told her I was doing a Christian work visiting homes in her area. She invited me to sit down across from her. She told me she had been very depressed as of late. She said she had just finished praying to God that if He didn't send a Christian by to help her within a half an hour, she was going to take her own life. She, Idora, added she had no work, no place of her own, and faced some health problems. A friend, who had taken her in, was doing the best he could.

I told her I was very glad the Lord had sent me by, and that I pray daily for the Lord to send me to the right homes. I told her my wife and I would like to visit her regularly and share hope with her from the Bible. She appreciated the offer and said she would like that. After talking for awhile longer, I gave her a small book, Steps to Christ, and then had prayer with her. When I left, she had a smile on her face. And I, of course, had a smile to give back to her.

Idora became a good friend and Bible student. She soon accepted Jesus as her Saviour and joined the Roanoke Seventh-day Adventist Church. She couldn't drive so a church member was faithful to take her to church. She didn't live but three years longer, but I was thankful for God's divine intervention that gave her hope for a beautiful life to come.

One other experience I'll never forget was at an old home in a rundown area of Roanoke. I knocked at the door and soon it opened just enough for a pistol to slide out that was aimed at my head. A man asked "What do you want?". With a calm voice (thanks to the Holy Spirit) I told him I did a Christian work and that he or someone had sent in a card wanting more information about our literature. The pistol remained steady as he said he hadn't done it. I then said that, if he didn't mind, I'd be glad to share about our program with him anyway. Surprisingly, he said "Come on in."

We ended up having a nice visit. But he never did explain the pistol. I left him some free literature and a Bible-study-by-mail enrollment card that he could send in when he liked. I had prayer with him and we parted as friends. I thanked the Lord again for His angels that watched over me day after day. And I also thanked Him for the privilege of doing a work which gave me opportunities to get to know Him better.

Chapter 11

A New Direction

We knew when we moved to Wirtz there was no Adventist church in that whole county (Franklin County). So we continued attending the Roanoke Church. I became an elder and a junior Sabbath School teacher and Betty worked with the younger classes. Soon, however, Betty was watching over a second son in Sabbath School. Travis Alan was born just 15 months after Shaun's birth. Renée had been praying for a baby sister, but she loved him anyway. I, of course, now had more responsibility for Shaun not only at church but also at home. He and I began to bond now better than ever. He was a boy from head to toe and loved to play and be outdoors. As he got older he and Renée pretended to be LEs, carrying my sales case through the house. Occasionally one of them would actually go with me on a short day.

Yes, children are precious. They are a God-given responsibility as well. That's one reason I liked my work – to encourage and equip parents to raise their children to be good citizens here as well as in heaven. It takes some time, but if time is limited, we need to make it a quality time. What better quality than reading life-changing Bible stories! And added to that home environment must be the church Sabbath School (or Sunday School) and its worship service. From this children get that needed support from their friends and their parents. It takes time because Satan works tirelessly to influence our children toward worldly interests; we must be just as persevering.

Where they attend school is vital as well. Some public schools are better than others, but none really can (or have the legal right to) run the school from a Christian perspective. It used to be that public schools were very moral and neutral in their world view. Today there are many world views competing for a voice in our schools, resulting in the Christian world view being shut out almost completely. This makes the home and church influence so much more important.

It also requires Christian parents to think seriously about church schools. Expensive as they seem to be getting, their value is also increasing, as the world morally slides down hill. We were blessed to have a Seventh-day Adventist church school in Roanoke. We began sending Renée there at the age of 7. I would take her as I went to work. This ride became part of my quality time with Renée. And then at her school I knew I was getting support for what Betty and I taught her at home. Adventists have these Christian schools (from kindergarten to university) all over our country, and presently have the largest Protestant church school system in the world.

About a year after Betty and I moved to Wirtz, we became involved in the start of a new Adventist church in Franklin County. We made a lot of friends in the county and we thought Roanoke was a little far to invite them to church. Providentially, an older Adventist couple (Jim and Eileen) moved into the county about the time we did and became wonderful partners with us as we stepped out in faith to establish a new church plant. The Lord then drew in a few other families and we were soon looking for a place to rent. And the Lord intervened again! When Jim contacted the Presbyterian Church in Rocky Mount, he found the pastor more than happy to allow us to meet there on Saturday mornings and Tuesday evenings. The pastor said he had once been a chaplain in the military and had worked closely with some Adventist medics who performed a good, self-sacrificing work for his unit. He had always wanted to do something ever since to show his appreciation for Adventists. So, the Presbyterian Church charged us no rent for about 6 years (we did pay for the increase in utilities), after which we moved into our own new building. God loves to reward good service for Him. Many times, though, we never see the results.

Through the years, many in Betty's family came to the Lord and joined the Adventist Church. Her mom and sister, Alyce, joined when Betty did in California. Later, sisters, Billie and Vicki, and brothers, Eager and John, and lastly her dad, Howard at 80, were all baptized. Betty has 2 other siblings as well, a Baptist and a Mormon. Ever since leaving home after high school this family has been scattered all over the USA. For years, letters and phone calls were the primary way they stayed in touch. Now that many are Adventist, there is an additional bond between them, and all are part of God's family too.

When we become a member of God's family, it's His intention that we all work together in sharing the gospel and uplifting humanity. The Bible says we are all given special spiritual gifts (talents) that enable us to work together to do this. The apostle Paul likens it to the many parts of the body, all performing a different function for the benefit of the body. The Adventist Church has many different "parts" that serve the primary goals of sharing the gospel and uplifting humanity.

One area of interest that the Lord has given Betty and me from the time we joined the church has been that of physical health, as well as spiritual health. We've strived to learn and incorporate good nutrition and lifestyle principals into our lives and also share these with others. This goal has naturally led us to a plant-based diet and away from heavily processed foods. God has blessed this plan for our lives by giving us and our children excellent health. We, at the beginning, were quite zealous in sharing this health interest with others, whether they wanted to hear it or not. We naively felt everyone was ready to learn how to live differently and improve their health. We've had to ask for forgiveness from different ones whom we had offended.

Betty's brothers, John and Eager, were, as early Christians, also interested in health and rightly understood it as part of the overall gospel message. Jesus was as much involved in improving people's health and uplifting humanity as He was in sharing the plan of salvation. In fact, Jesus showed how these two parts of the gospel are to be carried out simultaneously. Meeting people's physical needs creates a desire in them to learn and accept Jesus for their spiritual needs. But also, as we allow Jesus into our heart, we, like Him, become compassionate toward the needs of others and seek ways to help.

A couple weeks before Memorial Day in 1977 John and Eager called to ask if they could come for a visit that holiday weekend. They wanted to talk over some ideas that they had been sharing on how to tie health and evangelism work together. Eager and his wife, Clara, were presently working with a health ministry (using natural remedies) at Uchee Pines Institute in Alabama. John was working as a computer programmer and looking for a closer involvement in the gospel work. We were glad for them to come, so the three came for a nice, long weekend visit. They described their desire to start a health ministry near a larger city, and use it to educate and help people toward better health. In this ministry they wanted to win the friendship and confidence of people so that spiritual things might be shared with them along the way. We agreed with them that many Americans are uninterested in attending Bible studies or evangelistic meetings, and that the health work can often break down the barriers toward God's plan of salvation and restoration.

That weekend we all prayed and talked a lot about combining a health and spiritual ministry. Adventists in other areas have used clinics, restaurants, bakeries, natural food stores, organic farms or gardens, nursing homes, lifestyle retreats, etc. as a way to serve the public and make friends. Near the close of the weekend the three of them asked Betty and me if we would support them in a similar type of work in the Roanoke area, in whatever the Lord led them to do. We said we would. We knew it would be great to have them living nearby and doing a Christian ministry together.

Eager and Clara were the first to arrive. John didn't want to quit his job until something began to come together. They moved in with us for a few days while they looked around the rural areas not far from Roanoke. They wanted a peaceful country spot, but not too far from town where they could easily connect with people. Not many days after they arrived though, we were informed that the owners had decided to sell the home we were renting. So, it now was two families looking for a home.

I was still working, of course, as an LE and so I let Eager and Clara do most of the looking at home possibilities. One day he reported that he had found an empty older house on what was once a dairy farm. It was on a dirt road near Boones Mill, not far from where we were living. It included a large acreage (around 125 acres) and was owned by a medical doctor in Salem, VA. He wanted to sell the whole place, but was willing to rent the house for now. It seemed big enough for Eager and Clara and us, and we could help them by sharing the rent.

Eager, I'm sure, was praying what he was to do now. He had been baking bread at Uchee Pines and had done some research and testing into how to make an all whole wheat bread that would rise well, have a soft texture, and taste good. He felt he had come up with a good recipe, and a good recipe it was, for it led to an amazing series of divine interventions in the next few months.

Chapter 12

A Miracle Bakery

In Exodus chapter 4 Moses was feeling helpless to the big task God was calling him to do, that of leading the Israelites out of Egypt. In verse 2 God asked Moses what he had in his hand. Moses said he had a rod; he was a shepherd at the time. God implied that was all he would need to lead the Israelites out of Egypt. When he asked Moses to cast it to the ground, it turned into a serpent, and then back into a rod. In other words, God was showing that He would supply the power.

Eager knew this story and other Bible examples of God's leading. So he began to use "what he had in his hand", a bread recipe. He made some whole wheat dough by hand and used the kitchen oven to bake it. Then he started giving out samples to us and to neighbors and friends. Everyone thought it was the best whole wheat bread they had tasted. And back in 1977 there just weren't many varieties of 100% whole wheat bread from which to choose. So Eager asked me (the salesman?) to take a few loaves along with me in my LE work. I did and I got the same positive response from lots of people. Everybody wanted more.

None of us knew where this was going to lead. But Eager wanted to go forward. He was able to get a well-used, modest-sized mixer (with a dough hook) and some pizza ovens from Uchee Pines. He started making bread in larger amounts that I was to sell during my day. Strange as it seemed, I was much more successful at selling bread now than books. I continued to make LE visits but the sales were quickly tapering off. And I began selling enough bread to be paid by the bakery account. It was a strange turn of events, but I could see the Lord leading in this new still-unknown venture.

I began the bread sales to people I already knew, many of whom were previous contacts through my LE work. They seemed happy to see me again, and surprised at my new product. Who ever heard of a door-to-door bread salesman? But everyone liked the bread and wanted me to return, and when I did they would have a neighbor or friend who also wanted some. Eager, since he had gotten the pizza ovens, was making his bread in quart juice cans so he could get more loaves in the oven. This added to the novelty of our bread. It was softer, having only a small end with a crust, and it was so easy to slice.

I developed a delivery system whereby I went to a certain area of the Roanoke Valley on a certain day and formed a delivery route that I would follow again two weeks later. I set up eight routes, four each in two successive weeks. Then I would start all over again. One of those routes was through Franklin County where we lived. Eager, early on, began making new varieties of whole wheat bread: Sunflower Oat, Raisin, and Cashew Date. This added to the daily sales to the point I was now retailing over 150 loaves per day. And it wasn't long until I was also selling to the Natural Foods Coop in Roanoke, a big purchaser.

One of my retail customers was a Roanoke Times newspaper reporter. We became good friends. One day he asked me if we would mind having him come out to the farmhouse for the purpose of doing a story about our home bakery business. The family all agreed for him to come for a visit. I was delivering bread that day, but they all told me it was a wonderful warm visit. He brought his professional photographer with him, and he took pictures of children and adults. Betty, Eager, Clara, and Jack (Clara's brother who had joined us) were all interviewed and shared the vision and purpose of our work, and giving God the glory through it all. The reporter liked the back-porch setup for the bakery as well as our quiet country setting for raising our kids. Brother John still hadn't joined in our work yet, but he was supporting us with his prayers, finances, and encouragement. However, he was to be added to our labor force in the near future.

Very soon after the reporter's visit, there appeared a full-page article about Eden Way Bakery on the front page of Section C in the large Sunday edition of The Roanoke Times. "Eden Way" was now our chosen name because it helped people to think about the simple, original diet God had chosen for humans from the beginning. The article was well written, descriptive, and had several large attractive pictures included; one of the equipment with bread in the making, one of the bakers, and one was a close-up of our youngest son, Travis, holding a slice of bread to his mouth with a bite already taken out. The article presented a warm, caring family working together to provide a healthful service to the community. No better advertising could have been purchased at any price. Only God could cause this to happen!

And this wasn't the end of the story. Starting the next day, Monday, I was continually being stopped by people who had read the article and wanted to try the bread too. They would see me making a delivery to a house and would call out that they wanted some too. Sales doubled to 1100-1200 loaves per week. Kroger started ordering bread as did the Nature's Outlet which had two health food stores in the Valley. John now had to join our team in the kitchen. It was starting to get cramped: people, flour and ingredients, and finished bread everywhere, ready for delivery the next day. The flour was stacked in Eager and Clara's bedroom. At night we would kid them by saying "Wheat dreams!"

God was soon going to resolve the space problem. We got a call from Hollin's College, now Hollin's University, near Roanoke. They had read our Sunday newspaper article and were wondering if we might be interested in some equipment they had that they weren't using anymore. They needed the space more than the equipment, and this included a large rotary oven, a walk-in cooler, and a reach-in cooler. They had been used in pottery classes the college had offered and they were still in good working order. And the amazing thing was that they didn't want a dime for it. It was heavy equipment, and they would be pleased if we would just come and take it out. We gladly agreed, not yet knowing where we might use it. So, on pick-up day, Eager and John stored this equipment in the barn across from the farmhouse. We knew the Lord must have plans for it soon.

So, they began "in their free time" to check for a possible new location for our bakery. It wasn't long until they found a nice brick building with a space to rent right on Route 220 north of Rocky Mount. The owner, who had a garage next door, was a very pleasant, amiable man. He was quite agreeable to all the changes that had to be made to make the space into a bakery. And, praise to the Lord, it housed perfectly the oven, coolers, mixers, molding machine, bread slicer, tables, and proofing box (a complete bakery) with room for a small store at the front. And we were debt free! Then a large, attractive, black and yellow Eden Way Bakery sign was placed atop the building, easily visible from the 4-lane highway. Only the Lord could arrange all this. We used this facility for 12 years.

Sale of bread continued well. But some competitive good whole wheat breads were entering the market. We were able to get a used bun machine, which was used to make burger buns and dinner rolls. Eager also started making various kinds of whole grain cereals. And we packaged up bakery ingredients and I sold them along with the bakery products. So my car was quite full when I would leave for my deliveries. Eager, ever inventive, also began bread shipments, using United Parcel Service (UPS), to natural food stores in cities within a 1-day delivery time period. UPS trucks would stop by the bakery at the end of the baking days to pick up boxes of bread which would then be delivered the next day to retail stores across Virginia and into North Carolina.

At our new location, Eager and Clara met regular customers who became friends. Some wanted to learn more about good nutrition and food preparation. So evening classes were arranged for them and others to learn and get some hands-on experience. Eager and Clara would also accept offers to give talks and classes at other locations. Betty was a good support when she could be free from the care of our three children. My extra time was spent in developing a large garden near the farmhouse. There were 2-3 acres that I eventually worked into gardening use. The Lord had certainly provided well for this too.

Nearing the fall of 1978, Eager informed us that he was feeling a call to study for the ministry. He wanted to be more full-time in the Lord's work. He applied to Southern Adventist College, now Southern Adventist University. He was accepted and made plans to leave for school quickly. John also was making plans to go to California, where he eventually met his wife. Betty and I felt no call to go anywhere. The Lord had done so much to get us where we were that we couldn't entertain a thought about closing down. It would be a real step in faith for us to continue on, but we knew the Lord would not forsake us. He would provide the help we needed. And we knew that the farm was a wonderful place for our children, their pets, gardening, and nature walks. We also wanted to continue helping with our new church plant in Rocky Mount.

But to keep this work going I would have to learn to bake, a brand new venture for me. Eager had the recipes and baking process down in a nice, orderly fashion. In rather short order, I was a baker. The Lord was good to us as we moved forward, supplying us with good part-time help, some local and some from individuals joining us from afar. Many of them were temporary, but the Lord would then have a replacement. Our employee who worked the longest was a young, local, single Adventist (about 17 when he started) who needed work, job training, and life mentoring. I felt God asking me to hire him. He learned well and was a very dependable employee for about 12 years. We've been friends ever since.

Of course, when I went into baking I had to reduce my time on the road doing deliveries. So now I began to bake, box up the UPS deliveries, and load up my car on Mondays, do my deliveries early Tuesday (now more wholesale than retail) and come back to run the bakery's store in the afternoon, and repeat this schedule on Wednesdays and Thursdays. Friday was when I made granola and other cereals. It was a full week but I was still young and healthy. And I enjoyed meeting people in town and at the bakery. I made a lot of friends and always had literature to share with people about health and spiritual questions. Betty was my bookkeeper and treasurer. We were (and still are) a good team.

I have a fairly strong entrepreneurial spirit and this work suited me fine for now. As my boys got older (even at 5 and 6) they wanted to help in the bakery. This was great too, because this was good quality time with them. Their first work was helping to shape the dough after it was cut on the table. It was an average height table, but the boys were still so small they had to stand on buckets to do their work. From the beginning I paid them a little and it got to be more as they got older and took on more responsibilities. From this they learned to tithe, save, and spend well their money. They are married with families now and still are good managers of their money. If all parents could give their children useful responsibilities, and some monetary reward with it, they would see (with some mentoring) some good results in later years.

Chapter 13

God Leads in the Farm Purchase

As Betty and I were deciding to take over the bakery, we also had to make the big decision as to whether we should stay on the farm and buy it, if possible. The first year of renting had just ended. We told the doctor (owner) that we would love to buy the farm, but we still had little means to do so. He said he would be willing to lease for a year with the option to buy and (amazingly) have 90% of the rent money go toward the down payment. Plus, during the year, we could profit however we could from the farm and use all this money toward the down payment. This was an unheard of addition in a lease agreement. This farm (listed as 125 acres ±) had 75% of its property in forest. We asked him straight forward if this included any profit from wood cutting. The doctor said that it did. As a former forester I knew there was some valuable standing timber on the property. I also knew we most likely would not get the down payment without this provision. So, it seemed clear that God was going to be working for us to buy the farm. It was surely a divine intervention.

Our next step was to decide on a woodcutter. We wanted one

who would be careful what he cut and how he cut it. We certainly didn't want it clear cut. We preferred that just the mature trees be cut, and leaving younger ones more space and time to mature. I felt there were enough roads in the woods already so that logs could be cut up in the forest and then dragged out with cables. This should be done carefully so as to prevent erosion (the forested part was hilly). After some search God led us to just the man. He agreed with how we wanted it cut and gave a good fair price for the timber he would cut.

That fall he began taking truck loads of logs off the farm. Our elderly neighbors, who used to run the farm as a dairy, were sure we shouldn't be allowed to do this. They insisted we ask the doctor again if this was legal. Their questions put a question again in our minds, so we asked the doctor once more. And again he said this was his original agreement. So these neighbors (and I'm sure others too) watched with amazement as a lot of nice timber was harvested. We would remind them that "our God is an awesome God". The timber cutter did a very professional job. The forest hardly looked like it had even been cut.

I don't remember the amount we needed for the down payment, but at the end of the lease year we were still a little short of being able to make the purchase. Betty and I were debating between us as to how to tell this to the doctor. We kept putting it off. Then one day the doctor came to talk to us. He asked us if we would be willing to delay the purchase one more year, with 90% of our rent money still going to the down payment. He said it would benefit him tax wise. We kindly told him we'd be glad to, and we breathed a big sigh of relief. God had blessed again. We were able to make the purchase the following year. Although the mortgage payment was larger than the rent payment, God always provided for us.

It wasn't long until Renée had finished high school and left to work and live with friends. Very soon after, the boys were of high school age, and being of a more spiritual nature, were willing to go to an Adventist boarding academy. We chose, with their approval, Little Creek Academy in Knoxville, TN. It had high social, spiritual, and academic standards and a good work program that helped students financially. The down side was that it was 5 hours away. We all shed tears when it was time to take them to enroll, but we felt it was the best decision for them. They did very well there; they appreciated the faculty, as well as the academic and work program. They were well prepared for college, for life, and for continued spiritual growth.

For Betty and me, the higher mortgage payment and helping with the boys education made our budget even tighter. We were also giving toward what would soon be a new church in Rocky Mount. But we had stepped out in faith and God blessed accordingly. At different times when money was short, which seemed at tax time, a neighbor would knock on our door wanting to know if we would be interested in selling a few acres on our border which we weren't needing anyway. And this would keep us going for another couple years. We trusted God was in control.

Chapter 14

A New Broader Venture

The bakery was still doing well and our big garden did well each year. I sold some vegetables on my deliveries, but Betty canned a lot of our vegetables and the fruit we picked at local orchards. She was so good at keeping our food expenses low. I believe the vegetarian route is the cheaper way to eat and Betty's work made it even more economical. She has also been good at natural home treatments for health problems and this kept our medical expenses super low. Betty was proof that a stay-at-home mom can more than pay her way, especially when I consider her work as our bakery bookkeeper and treasurer. She also found time to offer nutrition and natural foods cooking classes to community and church groups.

Around 1986, a couple from northern Virginia, Lou and Barb (and their 5 children) inquired about buying some property because they wanted to move to the country. We showed them the top of the hill on one side of the farm. It was what they wanted and they bought 30 acres. They originally were put in touch with us by a mutual friend who knew Lou and Barb had an interest in natural foods restaurant work (possibly in Roanoke) and our friend felt we could join forces. So we began meeting and discussing how and where we could do this. Since Lou and I were both working, it took some time for this to move forward. Betty's brother, John, had moved back in the area with his new wife, Sally, and they too got into these discussions. We needed a man like John in on it because he has work skills to make things happen. But it's always fun to dream, gain a vision, and see if and how the Lord opens doors for it to happen.

Of course Betty was listening in too. And when she realized that we might be moving our bakery and store into Roanoke, and that Franklin County (and Rocky Mount) would then have no natural food store, she started thinking how she (herself) could open up a natural foods store in Rocky Mount. There was a new shopping center just opening up in Rocky Mount and Betty and I thought "wouldn't it be wonderful if we could have a store right in the middle of that new shopping center, the best place in town". We began making plans (stepping out in faith) and, wouldn't you know, another Adventist couple wanted to move into our area and bought 5 acres, making it possible for Betty's dream to come true. We got the middle of that shopping center too! God is able! Betty enjoyed managing that store for about 7 years. Rent was high but the Lord provided faithfully.

Meanwhile John and Sally, Lou and Barb, and I continued to discuss a joint venture of our bakery and natural foods store with his planned vegetarian café. Lou, already well employed, was going to be the financial backer. Sally and Barb agreed to be the chefs, and John would direct the physical move and set up. I would manage the bakery and store. It seemed like a good team. We found an empty store front in Roanoke's downtown city market. These openings seldom happened and would be filled quickly when they did. The city market is a busy place, and a well-known tourist stop. The area includes a vibrant farmer's market, lots of craft stores, and a wide variety of restaurants. And it is within easy walking distance from many major downtown businesses and the employees find this area a welcome lunch break. So we felt very blessed to be there.

It took a few months to prepare the building for the needs we had. We named our new business "Eden Way Place". It looked bright, clean, and cheery when we opened up. The store was at the front, the open café behind it, and the bakery and café seating area were side by side behind the café kitchen area. The café seating area, however, was elevated about 3 feet, giving customers a nice full view of the bakery and café in operation. The café was open 11:00 a.m. to 3:00 p.m. and the early customers were able to observe a lot of the baking process going on, along with the slicing and bagging of the bread. One product I began making when we moved to Roanoke was pita bread. It was so fun for people to watch a thin, round slice of dough going in our extremely hot little convection oven and then see it shortly puff up into a little balloon.

The café menu was completely vegan. Sally and Barb were experts at vegan cooking and their food made a hit from the beginning. We offered soups, salads, sandwiches, entrées, drinks, including carrot juice, desserts, and our bakery products. We made lots of friends, gave some interesting health classes, and shared a lot of personal advice and instruction. Sally and Barb were both gifted in teaching how to achieve better health. Our store was open 9:00 a.m. to 5:00 p.m. and was one of the many unique shops in the market that people liked to visit. Just as I had done at the previous location, I ordered some natural foods in bulk and would repackage them into smaller quantities. We offered the more natural dietary supplements and a good variety of books on health, nutrition, and vegetarian cooking. It's always satisfying to encourage people to eat more healthfully and enjoy a fuller life.

The Bible speaks of our body being "the temple of the Holy

Spirit which dwells in us" and, because we have been "bought with a price" (through Jesus' death), we should "therefore glorify God in our body and our spirit which are God's" (1 Corinthians 6:19, 20). Science has proven that many of our body's diseases are due to poor nutrition and faulty lifestyle as well as a discontented spirit toward life and others. With Jesus directing our lives, we gain a new positive outlook toward life and desire to live more healthfully to His glory. And it was our privilege to guide people in this new purpose for living. I remember a young Jewish man who became a regular customer. He ran a pawn shop in the market area. He came in out of curiosity at first but it wasn't long until he was a great promoter of the café. At first, he had a sullen spirit but later he was so cheerful and amiable. I believe our Eden Way Place was a "breath of fresh air" for a lot of down-trodden and overworked people. In addition to good food and friendship, we had good Christian instrumental music playing during work hours.

We met people from all over the world: Russia, Eastern Europe, England, Africa, Australia, and Latin America. It made the day special to talk with them about their home, work, and families. They enjoyed watching our baking and cooking taking place and learning how we Americans did it. They always left as friends whom we hoped to meet one day again in heaven. How nice heaven will be, where there will be no goodbyes.

We operated our "Place" for 5 years. But as you probably know, this type of work takes its toll on many workers. There is pressure to please, to meet time schedules, and to make a profit. We lost some of our workers and got replacements, but they were "employees" and didn't have the vision or purpose that we had at the beginning. The rent went up yearly, but our sales remained stable or fell a little. This became a financial crunch so the majority chose not to sign the lease for the 6th year. The last cook (a good one), Tom, bought some of the equipment to open a smaller "Eden's Way Café" on the market as a private business. He continued our health name for a good number of years.

This also seemed to be the end for the bakery as well. I had mixed feelings. It had always been long hours with only a modest income from it. But with God's constant interventions along the way, it always seemed to be a joy. It had been a special blessing to our family, a real growing-together experience. And I believe the community was blessed as well. I know my faith and Betty's faith were strengthened greatly. If that alone was the reason for these 17 years of labor, it was worth it. But I have to admit I cried as I saw all the equipment going in different directions. It seemed that my life was splitting up, and that I would be out of work!

But God hadn't left me. He says "Lo, I am with you always, even unto the end of the world" (and that included my world.) Everyone goes through times of disappointment and sorrow, but faith in God will keep us from giving up. There is a line in a Christian song that says "He hasn't brought us this far to leave us". So I began praying for where the Lord wanted to lead us now. Life is meant to be a series of steps, each one taking us a little higher in service to the Lord. I soon began to sense what that next step was.

Chapter 15

A New Calling

The Lord knows the end from the beginning. Before we were even near the closing of Eden Way Place, circumstances had led us to sell more property and pay off our mortgage. A large portion was sold through an auction on a Veteran's Day Monday. As the farm was being surveyed prior to the auction, it was discovered the actual area of our farm was 175 acres, not the 125± that was on the deed. How awesome! It made me think back when Betty and I were giving heavy to the new church and putting the boys through academy. We occasionally had to sell land to pay year end taxes. And this had made me a little discouraged; I was giving to the Lord but coming up short. Now the Lord was telling me I had nothing to worry about. He already knew we had an additional 50 acres, more than what we had sold for taxes. You can't out give the Lord!

The surveying divided the property into several large tracts. The going price was much lower than I had hoped, but it was enough to pay off our mortgage. John had bought 15 acres at the top of the hill, and a realtor bought one tract, and our adjoining neighbor bought the rest. We later sold the barn and its acreage to a local man who had golden work horses. The farmhouse and its five acres were also sold, going to a man and his new bride who completely refurbished the inside. The "extra" 50 acres were divided and sold at a later date, but there was one 5-acre tract that no one seemed to want; everyone said "where would you put a house?" Betty and I could see where it could go. So we put in a short drive, dug for a basement, and bought a nice, new modular home to put on that basement. And this was where we were living (debt free) when Eden Way Place was closed.

So, now as I was praying for the Lord to lead, I felt a strong urge to enter the ministry. But at my age (53) I didn't want to go back to school. As it is in some other denominations, a person in the Adventist Church can sometimes find pastoral positions as a lay pastor. For sometime I had been getting a monthly lay worker newspaper which included such opportunities within our church. As I was scanning it some months before we closed, I noticed an advertisement for a lay pastor in Austin, Minnesota, of all places. There were no others being advertised. Betty certainly had questions as to whether this could be for us. She is a Southerner through and through, having been raised near Bristol, Virginia. To her, Minnesota was like saying the North Pole. We also had Renée, her husband, and baby boy now living in the area nearby. The boys were in college in Tennessee. "Why would the Lord want us to even consider moving up there?"

On the other hand, I have to tell you that Betty is usually ready for new adventures. And so she let me make the call to Austin, MN. Sure enough the position was still open. The man (Linden McNeilus) said he was starting a new church plant for that area. He had already hired a good gardener to set up a pick-your-own vegetable garden that would help in getting acquainted with people. Linden was big into a scrap iron, recycling business, and he was financing this venture. He invited Betty and me to come up for a visit over Memorial Day Weekend. We decided to go. We left Boones Mill in very nice weather, and arrived in Dodge Center (where he lived) in rainy 45 degree weather. We shivered!

Linden was an older man, past retirement age, and married. He seemed set on starting this church before he fully retired. He had bought 3 homes near the garden area at Austin to house his workers in this project. He introduced us to the gardener, Earl, and his family and to the work that Earl had already done in the small greenhouse and the garden. Linden said that I would be working in the garden and also be the spiritual leader as everything moved forward. Linden was also opening up a retail outlet for his scrap iron at the garden area that would help fund this project. I enjoyed gardening and sales, and had helped start a church before, so the program interested me. We told Linden we would pray about it and let him know.

Betty and I drove back to Virginia discussing this opportunity. I told her that the timing seemed to make it appear that this was a beginning for me into lay pastor work. We prayed for a few days and I still felt the Lord calling me there. He wasn't opening any other doors. So, we called Linden and he encouraged us to come on up. A couple weeks after that telephone call was when Eden Way Place officially closed. We loaded up a large U-Haul truck and our two cars, said some emotional goodbyes, and headed north. We were again stepping out in faith. It was early July and certainly warm when we arrived this time.

As I said, Linden was an older man. I guess between when we had visited him and when we had called him back, he had mistakenly hired another Alan and his wife, thinking it was me calling him back. Anyway, he was embarrassed but wanted to keep us both. He had also hired a secretary and a young Russian fellow, out of the goodness of his heart, who needed work. So we had plenty of help! The garden was going strong by the time we had returned. Linden was also keeping us busy setting up his open-air retail scrap iron shop. We even laid down some concrete sidewalks around the area.

But Betty and I also began to take some time going into town to get acquainted with different agencies and social work that was going on. We wanted to see how we could fit in with some type of community service. We found a lot of friendly people. One of the friendliest was a little Adventist lady Mrs. Carlson. She was so glad to have us stop by to see her occasionally. The closest church for her was over 20 miles away, so she didn't get many church family visits. She still drove to her church herself. I think she felt that to attend our little church gathering would be "disloyal" to her home church.

One unique thing about Austin we will never forget is the terrible smell. It is the home of Hormel Meats. A big slaughter house is very near town and we hated to go through that section. But a breezy day could take that smell for miles in any direction. It occasionally reached our gardens, maybe 4-5 miles away. But people were used to it and it smelled like money to them. But I have wondered how many people have become vegetarians after visiting Austin.

One of our outreach projects for the community was sharing a video series by Gary Smalley and John Trent on "Loving, Lasting Relationships". It emphasized improving marriage and family relationships. We rented an empty store front in a shopping center. We advertised and got a nice group out each night. Following each showing we had good discussions using the prepared questionnaire sheet. Betty and I were the first to admit that it helped our marriage relationship. We have our own video set now and have shared it with others and they, too, have been blessed. Surely you would agree that even good relationships can be improved. A happy, loving marriage in today's world is a wonderful influence for good and gives God glory.

We had free housing while we were in Austin. But we shared

our quarters with the business office (at the front) and with the young Russian man, who lived in the basement. He was a friendly fellow, still learning his English. Betty gave him some good help in getting his "green card" so he could get some work and continue his studies. I liked our housing arrangement; it was close to work and I was outside most of the time. But Betty began wishing she had her own private home. Our modular home in the woods back in Virginia was on the market but hadn't sold yet. We began praying more earnestly for the house to sell. And expecting it to sell soon, Betty started looking at homes in the area. She saw one or two that she liked but we had to keep putting it on hold.

For our first year, our community garden did very well. A fair number of town people came to pick their own produce. We had a good variety, but sweet corn seemed the favorite. We had to work extra hard to get the sweet corn through some severe thunderstorms. Several times the high winds flattened the stalks and then we would have to go stand each one back up again. The farmers' field corn never seemed to be affected. The roots of field corn are apparently much deeper. As an Easterner, some of these storms were frightening to me; the dark rolling clouds looked massively dangerous. I was thankful that I never saw a tornado.

Our eggplant crop did exceptionally well, but it wasn't a favorite of the local people. So we had nice eggplant in excess. Betty hates to see anything go to waste, so she pulled together some of her eggplant recipes from her files (like eggplant Parmesan) to share with people. And she quickly created some new ones like eggplant cookies and pie. And of course, she made some to share with others, and so we all enjoyed them. Eggplant is something like tofu in that it takes on the flavor of the other ingredients.

Linden's scrap steel outlet was a new experience for me. He had small and large, and long and short, of every imaginable shape of individual metal pieces. People far and near knew where to go for a plate or bar to fix something. What was scrap to most people was just what someone else needed. Business was picking up as summer turned into fall. But our garden and scrap steel sales weren't able to support the number of people Linden had hired. I knew it concerned him a lot because he was picking up the tab. But, for starting out, business still seemed quite promising. Earl was planning on expanding into fruits (even kiwis) and berries.

By mid-autumn Betty and I noticed that Linden's mental and physical health was noticeably deteriorating. He would repeat things he had told us before. His temperament seemed a little harsher. Then, one day in mid-December, the bad news came that Linden had had a severe stroke. We knew it would affect our work there because he was the financial support. Linden's Adventist sons also had big businesses in Dodge Center but their giving was for world mission programs of the church. They were never real excited about their dad's local project in Austin.

When we met with the family a few days later, we were told that, considering Linden's age and severity of the stroke, he was not expected to recover much. There would be lots of expenses, so they were deciding to close the Austin project. They expressed regrets for having to do so. They said they would pay each family $1000 to help cover moving expenses to wherever we chose to go. This, of course, was a sudden end to a lot of plans and dreams. Losing work happens to a lot of people today in our down-turned economy, but it wasn't so common back in 1995. Our little group were people of faith, so none of us experienced great anxiety for the future. But we were disappointed that we had to break up our team and end our vision for a new church. We spent some time thinking about what we had gained by this short time together. One thing Betty and I agreed we had gained was a better and more spiritual approach in our marriage. The big message from the Smalley-Trent videos was that we need to look to God to meet our needs and not put that pressure on our spouse. This seems common sense to a Christian, but in reality it isn't practiced so much.

We expect our spouse to fill all the holes in our life. Only God can do that. Many marriages could be saved and be much happier if this principle were practiced.

We were so glad now that our home in Virginia had not sold. We actually had a signed contract on the home a couple months earlier. But the buyers were going through a VA loan process that would take two months. At that time we moaned at another delay, but now we were so glad that it was a VA loan. Otherwise we might have bought a home by now and then had another home to sell, because we were now deciding not to stay in Minnesota. It was too far north for Betty and probably me too. Plus it was so far from western PA where my family all lived.

So the big question was "where would we go now". I didn't feel called to return to the Roanoke area. No work seemed to beckon me there. The new Adventist Church in Rocky Mount was well established and prospering. So, of course, we prayed a lot. I hoped to continue in work as a lay pastor. While we were waiting for divine direction, Betty wanted to visit her mother in Texas and then go visit a couple possibilities in the East. The McNeilus family wasn't hurrying us to move, so we just left in our car and drove to Alvin, TX near Houston. We had a wonderful time visiting her mom (it was a long time in coming) and her sister Vicki and husband, with whom her mom was living.

We then drove to Burlington, NC to visit some friends who wanted us to work on a health ministry that a church member was trying to start there. It was nice seeing our friends, but we didn't feel an open door there. So we drove on to western Pennsylvania to see my dad and others. My mom had died in 1989 and Dad (now 91) had been living alone ever since and doing well. It was nice to visit him; we saw him too rarely. The local church (in Gibsonia) very much wanted us to move to the area to help in their church leadership and outreach. We checked with the Pennsylvania Conference to see if there would be any lay pastor position available for me.

They said "not at this time".

But we did feel at one with the church. We knew a lot of them from previous visits when we came to see my family. Also, I felt drawn "to come home" to spend some quality time with my dad before he should die. So Betty and I decided to just come to Pennsylvania on faith that something would open up for us. This was really stepping out in faith and, as I had experienced many times before, God divinely intervened in the coming years.

Chapter 16

Entering Pastoral Ministry

Betty and I have often said, and only half joking, that she would never have agreed to leave warm Virginia to live in cold Pennsylvania if she hadn't first gone to colder Minnesota. It was February when we pulled our loaded Ryder truck and two cars into Dad's driveway. He had agreed we could live with him until we bought a home. We took most of our belongings to a rental storage unit nearby. It was nice for the two of us to spend time with Dad. Thirty five years had gone by since I had left home for college. Visits during that time had often been short. Now we were going to live nearby.

We began house hunting since our house in Virginia had sold. We preferred to live in the Cranberry Township area which was half way between Dad's home and the Gibsonia church we would be attending. Prices for homes were higher than they were in our part of Virginia. So we had to do some serious shopping if we wanted to stay debt free. We did some driving by homes for sale without our realtor. One day we drove through an average-priced neighborhood to check on some homes. One in particular was not so high priced, so we wanted to see it. As we drove up, a man was on a backhoe working on the sewer line between the house and street. The whole yard looked unsightly, so Betty told me to not even stop.

But my foot put on the brake anyway. Was it me or the Lord? I told Betty that while we were here we could at least look around. Well, we did. The house wasn't too impressive either. It was dark inside, poorly maintained, and smelled bad from animals and dampness. However, it had three bedrooms and two baths and with a wall removed it could have a lot more openness. But it wasn't worth the price they were asking. Betty was reluctant to go any further. But I thought the house had possibilities by doing some wall changes, upgrading the kitchen and bathrooms, painting, and carpeting. I could put in a French drain around the house to reduce the dampness. It was in a nice neighborhood, so it would make it more profitable to improve the house. But the sale price would have to be reduced for us.

The realtor thought we should just make a lower offer. But we first wanted to show it to an almost-retired couple from church who could give us their advice. After seeing it, they, too, thought the house had nice potential. They said they personally would be willing to help us in the renovation. So Betty became more convinced that maybe the Lord was the One that had put the brake on a few days before. We made a significantly lower offer, and the owner decided to take it.

Betty was already working a job she had been promised by a Gibsonia church member when we moved to the area. It was an accounting job that fit Betty's skills and interest. So now it was me and this house. This was another step in faith to be sure. But it was amazing how the Lord put me in touch with the right people, with the right skills, and with the right interest in what we wanted to do. I helped daily with arranging appointments, doing the painting, constant cleaning, and lots of unskilled work, as well as making smaller on-site decisions. The church couple lent their promised help too. But it took a lot of time, more than we had thought. Dad was gracious in letting us stay with him during all this time. But we finally did move into the home, and one would have hardly recognized it from the one we bought!

We were warmly welcomed at the local church. With my background they insisted I take the head elder position of the church starting in January. Their current head elder was moving to South Carolina soon. I accepted the position but I also accepted an invitation by the conference to start attending some church leadership training classes being held at the conference office in Reading. These continued on a periodic basis for a couple years and were a real blessing as I gradually took on more responsibilities. The Gibsonia church pastor was also pastor of a much larger church in Pittsburgh, and spent most of his time working there. This gave me opportunities for experience while I was doing my leadership classes. In the summer of 1998, he was instrumental in my getting a 3-month summer stipend to work with him in some special outreach and Bible work in the south side of Pittsburgh. I enjoyed it and we worked well together.

Our year-end newsletter that year to friends and family made mention of my interest in lay pastor work and that I had worked that summer for the conference. When our friend, Kingsley Whitsett, then president of the conference in West Virginia, read the letter, he immediately thought of a district near Beckley that we could fill. So he wrote us and invited us to consider being a pastor for the Welch district on a modest stipend. This seemed like the opportunity I wanted, but I wasn't thinking about going somewhere else. My hope was for something in our current area where I could conveniently visit with my dad. But then, I told myself, I need to put God's will ahead of my desires, even if they seem good. So Betty and I agreed we needed to at least check out the call and see if it seemed to be from the Lord.

So we drove down to the Welch church one Sabbath to meet Elder Whitsett and the members. I had the sermon for the church service and the Lord blessed me. Then we met the people over lunch and had a short get-acquainted meeting. We liked the people and felt quite warmly received. Elder Whitsett again gave us an invitation to come. Betty and I felt that the Lord was calling us there. But we told Elder Whitsett that we would pray about it and let him know.

When our home church in Gibsonia learned that we had been given a stipend call to go to West Virginia, the church leaders called the Pennsylvania Conference right away and asked them if they would be willing to hire me for a similar stipend to stay where I was. Surprisingly, they said they would. However, I would also have to take the Butler Church, which was 15 miles to the north. So I accepted the Pennsylvania invitation and told Elder Whitsett that I was sorry to have to turn him down. He said he understood.

So this was the beginning of my full-time ministerial work with the Adventist Church. I worked full time, even though paid on a stipend, because I enjoyed the work. I especially enjoyed making home visits to befriend and encourage members. I felt comfortable and able to do this because of my experience in literature evangelism. Many pastors do not visit in homes, and, instead, set up appointments for people to come to their office. This may seem a more efficient use of time, but it really isn't as effective. One can learn more, and accomplish more, in the home visit and the relationship is made stronger.

Attendance in the Gibsonia Church grew as time went on. And soon our sanctuary was filled close to capacity every Sabbath. But our greatest need was for Sabbath School classrooms; we were currently using a small library and the fellowship room as classes. The church probably had had plans to add classrooms, but it had never done so. So my suggestion was that we make a modest addition of two classrooms on the end. But a few members thought that it wouldn't cost too much more to put a basement underneath the addition and make the top level a new sanctuary. I had my reservations. It seemed like too big an undertaking for a small church. But the board voted to go with a new sanctuary and basement. So work began in earnest.

The Butler Church was renting a Presbyterian Church in town, and had been for maybe 15 years. They had once or twice looked into buying a building or church, but had not been able to find one that they could afford. I began checking into possibilities shortly after I took over the church. I found a nice-looking, old, stone church that was empty on the opposite side of town. It used to be a Catholic Church in the past. I asked our members about it and they said they had once asked about it a few years back. But the owner, a private individual, had said he had plans himself to renovate it into a community center. Well, nothing had been done yet.

So I went to visit him. He was a good-natured, elderly man and invited me in. He still had a strong interest in the building, wanted to see it restored, but he wasn't sure now if he could do it. His health was deteriorating. He would have to decide soon. I stopped by occasionally as a friend. His wife was in favor of him selling it to us. I told them both that we intended to use it for community use too. It would be a wonderful place for weddings, etc. Soon he relented and was willing to sell it to us at a price we could afford to fix it up. So work began in Butler too. I was busy now! But I was thankful that I had a top-notch builder from each church in charge.

If church attendance, support, and vision had continued where it had been in the Gibsonia Church, I'm sure the addition there would have been completed with flying colors. But two things happened that made the "roof cave in". One was unavoidable. In very close order we lost some good member families because of job transfers out of state. The other was a conflict among some members. This may have been partially fueled by rising financial pressures on the church. Satan used it to his best advantage. Two key families left and now we were struggling. I felt shaken to my boots. I had never seen a church fall so quickly. I prayed for strength and wisdom. I did my best to remain neutral and to counsel and pray with different members. My personal friendship didn't seem to help mend the riffs. It was discouraging. Had I made the right choice to get into the ministry? Should I consider resigning? What was my future anyway?

The builder in charge, Ron, (who had pushed for the new sanctuary) was still determined to see it finished. And he often needed a helper, which I agreed to be. We made good progress. It was now the summer of 2002 and I had just turned 60. One day I was standing on an eight-foot scaffold putting in drywall screws above my head when I blacked out and fell free-fall to the floor below. I didn't wake up until Ron was there trying to talk to me. I wasn't responding too well, so he quickly called the ambulance. He then called Betty to come to the church. I remember a little of the trip to Pittsburgh and the man trying to get me to answer questions. Betty and Ron were following in their cars.

We waited awhile in the ER and my mind started to clear up. Finally they put me in a room and the technicians started running a battery of tests for the next couple days. I had fractures of the skull, a broken rib that punctured a lung, and a broken collar bone and shoulder blade. All this would only require time and a little physical therapy to heal. Nothing was determined as to why I blacked out. All my tests showed that I was healthy, except for some arthritis in my neck. So, most likely some vessel or nerve got pinched in my neck when I was looking up too long.

I was home from the hospital in 4-5 days, but in quite a bit of pain. I almost lived in my favorite recliner chair for a couple weeks, day and night, except when I went to physical therapy. My taste buds were "damaged" so that food didn't taste good, even some of my favorites. Life has its bumps in the road. But I wasn't depressed because I only had to think what could have resulted from the fall. I could have fallen head first. I still thank the Lord and my angel that I fell on my left side.

The Pennsylvania Conference, thankfully, didn't lose faith in me through all this. I praise the Lord for His patience too. Once I was on my feet again (barely), I was called to pastor the district just to the north (and still not too far from my dad). With this call I was put on salary as a licensed minister. I was surprised and so appreciative. This new district was a 2-church district as well, but the two churches were 60 miles apart. But I only went to each church twice a month, so it worked out well. I thought Betty and I fit in pretty well in the first two churches (and we did), but we seemed to fit even better with these two churches. We spent almost six years there in enjoyable service and evangelism. I continued to grow spiritually and in abilities to serve God's people.

We had to rent at first, until our house sold in the previous district. We wanted to live somewhere between the two churches, so, before moving we looked at possible locations. Then Betty went by herself to look for rental options. At Titusville she decided to put a classified ad in the paper that would get us in touch with homes for rent. The lady at the newspaper desk said Betty was too late for the upcoming paper but she would hold it for the next issue. Shortly after Betty left, a man from Pleasantville (close by) came in with an ad about a house for rent. A little surprised, the lady at the desk mentioned Betty's advertisement that had just been brought in. She was kind enough to give the man, Gilbert, our telephone number.

The next day Betty took a call from Gilbert. After talking a bit about the rental home and who we were, Betty offered that we could drive up Thursday to see him and the house. He mentioned that that was normally his golfing day, so Betty quickly said we wouldn't want to interfere with that; we could come a different day. Gilbert must have felt pleased at their conservation and this little courtesy because he then told Betty that he felt "we were the type of people he wanted to rent to". So the house was ours to rent, subject to our approval once we saw it. What a difference a little thoughtfulness makes in our rough and tumble world. Christians need to remember that others are looking to see what difference Jesus makes in our lives. The fruits of the Spirit are the measuring stick that they use.

Betty and I enjoyed our time in Gilbert's rental house. He lived next door and we became good friends with him and his wife. They weren't church goers but they were loving people. But, being retired, they always spent the winter in their second home in Myrtle Beach, SC. It was a smart habit, because that first winter was the most snow I ever experienced, 12-13 feet for the winter. We were living now in the Great Lakes snow-belt, plus Pleasantville sat on top of a small mountain range, and so it snowed there hard and often. But the snow-plowers were very capable and always on the job. I rarely missed getting out to work. I got a lot of good exercise shoveling our short driveway. Betty didn't complain; it wasn't as cold as Minnesota.

Our previous home sold in the spring. Betty was out house hunting before it was final. She really likes being a homeowner. She saw a cute smaller house in a newer, spacious subdivision nearby that was just going up for sale. We were the first, and subsequently the only ones, to whom the realtor showed the house. It seemed to be the house the Lord picked out for us. The price was right, the kitchen spacious, and a prevalent nice shade of blue paint throughout the house.

Though it was less than 5 years old, the price was lower because the basement was unfinished, though laid out for a couple of rooms. Our boys helped with completing this project when they came to visit. This new home was one of our favorites, a quality built home inside and out. Along with our now full-time pastoral work, we certainly felt blessed. I visited my dad regularly and enjoyed taking him shopping. He would soon be turning 100 years of age.

Chapter 17

Joys as a Pastor

One of the first things I did again in this new district was to visit everyone in their home. I learn so much about members this way. Most people love to talk about their past, especially the older folks, and it does them well to remember how God led them and provided for them in their walk through life. I learn what their talents and spiritual gifts are and what they prefer to do for the church. Sometimes they would give me names of people they wanted me to visit. I tried to encourage my church leaders to do the same with only limited success. People are too satisfied with the short visits at church. Friendships could be more and deeper if members visited each other in their homes or spent the day together at a park. We are to be "the family of God". Fellowship lunches after church can be another good option, if we don't sit with the same people all the time.

In this district especially, I wanted Betty and me (and the churches) to be involved in the community. And the Lord blessed this desire abundantly. We had a non-Adventist friend who lived in Titusville that worked with the public school system. Her responsibilities included having annual health fairs in the high school to help students be more aware of healthy living. She, being health conscious, invited us to come and have one of the "stations" (or blocks of time) where students would come for 20-30 minutes to learn about that station's health emphasis. Students could choose which stations they wanted to attend that day.

We would have fun talking with them about good nutrition and its benefits, but we would also take a variety of samples for each student to try and even have them make one or two. They often asked good questions about things they had read or heard about healthful living. I remember sharing with them about a high school in Appleton, Wisconsin. This school was where all the harder to manage students of that county were sent to attend. It had a full-time policeman to help keep order and a secured entrance into the school. Still, fights would break out regularly. Attendance was not good and the learning rate was slow. Someone suggested that the school make a complete, healthier change in their lunch program and the snack machines. The diet changes not only included less fat, salt and sugar, but also no artificial preservatives, colorings, or food enhancements. School officials agreed to try it. As they made the changes, they explained to students and parents why they were doing it. And they began doing it at home too. Within days the school became a different environment. There was no more violence; the policeman eventually lost his job. Student attention went up, as did the grades on the next report card. And attendance increased. It certainly hit the local paper as worthy news. I'm not sure why this hasn't grabbed more attention nationally. I guess special interest groups have a lot of influence in preventing these types of changes.

However, these local high school students were interested in what we shared, as well as the teachers who sat in on the presentations. The young are more ready for change, but the establishment often isn't. It works this way spiritually too. Most conversions take place in the younger years. Thankfully there are spiritual leaders who encourage young people to accept Jesus. I regretted I didn't have a lot of other public opportunities to connect with the younger generation.

However, through the Seneca Church we had a wonderful opportunity to meet the general public. Somewhat similar to when we opened the bakery years before, everything seemed to providentially come together to open up a vegetarian café in Oil City. The church was very supportive and helped make the place very attractive. Betty and the ladies worked up a good menu of soups, salads, sandwiches, smoothies, and some other tasty desserts. In the store section we included a nice selection of books and pamphlets for the family and marriage. So we called our café "The Lunch Box and Book Bag". The place had a most inviting atmosphere that one customer called it "a breath of fresh air". Our land lady was a real promoter for us and enjoyed coming in. But we seemed to have too few customers like her. I guess we were there before the local area was ready for it; a customer visiting from Philadelphia said she wished we were in her area.

We were open two years but the church had to regularly supplement our income. However, we got to meet a lot of nice people and did get involved in the community. We were invited to participate in Oil City's annual First Night event. This is a major event on New Years Eve promoted by the arts community. About 15 locations around town were selected to be a host site for a professional musical, art, or craft group to entertain the public. People would buy a ticket to spend New Years Eve visiting these different entertainment spots. It was good advertisement for the host sites because people would come far and near to attend First Night. They even had an "old trolley car" that would haul people from site to site if they couldn't walk. It was a festive night and a wholesome family event. Both years we hosted a couple who specialized making lots of animal and people figures from balloons they blew up. They would ask the kids "What would you like me to make for you?" And they would do it. It was so nice to see parents and their children enjoying fun and laughs together. It was a privilege to be part of First Night, and I thanked the Lord for this opportunity. I've since thought that it would be nice to have First Night events throughout our country. Lately, I've learned there are some other cities that do.

Our Lunch Box and Book Bag café was also invited to participate in a health fair in town a couple times. This is always a good time to meet people in other health related areas. We shared health literature, a few recipes, and some food samples from our menu. Much credit for our menu (and this whole enterprise) goes to Kim, a creative people-person. She was our manager and the PR person from the start. The church paid her a modest wage the first year, but because business didn't expand as we had hoped, we had to withdraw it. She then had to quit and seek other employment. Betty reluctantly became volunteer manager and did very well. I also had to volunteer more time the second year.

All in all, I consider the time and money for the café well spent. We sold a good amount of family books, DVDs, and CDs that we pray had lasting benefits. People were also trying some of our menu recipes in their homes. Coming to know the Lord and His "more abundant life" is a series of steps that people take. We were certain there were some (including our own members) who made a step or two during those two years the café was open.

In the town of Warren I became involved in prison ministries by volunteering time with the prison chaplain, John, whom I got to know through the ministerial association. He was a dedicated man in his spiritual service to the inmates, and was well liked by them. He invited me to go with him on Sunday nights. His wife would play the piano and 25 or more inmates would join in singing favorite hymns. Then a short sermon would follow, which I gave when I was able to be there. We always hoped their spiritual interest would continue once they were released. For some it did and that was gratifying.

I had quite a few funerals to conduct during my almost 6 years in the district. Some were not members of our church. Thankfully most of them were older people and the service could be more of a celebration of their life. I actually enjoyed these services. I could draw closer to the whole family in their time of need. And I always planned my sermonettes to be messages of hope in the love of God and Jesus' soon coming when families will be reunited. So my closing remarks would be for everyone to give their life to Jesus so that we can be a part of that grand reunion.

This reminds me of a time when I had three funerals in a short period of time. I started to experience significant tiredness and weakness. At first I thought I was suffering from too much stress and work time (and getting too old). Then one morning I noticed a large red blotch under one arm and down across my ribs. Betty thought this looked serious. She talked to a nurse, Hillerine, a Seneca Church member, who agreed with Betty and set me up with a doctor's appointment the very next day. This probably wouldn't have been possible without Hillerine's "pull". The next day the doctor took quite an interest in my skin rash. He said that he had just been reading an article about Lymes' disease that very morning. He said he had never seen an actual case, but from what he had been reading he thought this was it. It didn't have a fully developed "bull's eye" that most cases show, but a few don't.

The doctor was sure enough that he put me on an antibiotic that same day. He knew that the sooner it gets treated the more likely there will be a full recovery. But he wanted to be certain that it was Lymes' so he sent me to Erie the next day to see a specialist at the Infectious Disease Control office. The lady there agreed that it was, though the appearance wasn't typical. The antibiotics had to continue for two weeks, even though they brought my energy level up by the next day. I've since met people who weren't so blessed to have an early detection and they have had continual low energy problems. To me this certainly was a divine intervention, enabling me to get such quick detection and healing. I thank the Lord for it.

The most enjoyable and uplifting event for a pastor is baptism. This is the culmination of a series of divine interventions in a person's life. I had the privilege of conducting a fair number of baptisms during my ministry in Pennsylvania. God was so good to me. One of my favorites was an older gentleman by the name of Lewis Flatt who lived near Warren. He had been raised by Seventh-day Adventist parents but when he was about 18, he married a good Methodist girl and from that time on they always went to her church. They had a good long marriage, but he never forgot his roots. When she died, he began to think more about his upbringing. He told me how he liked Sabbath School and giving offerings for missionary work. One Sabbath his parents had no money for an offering and decided he should stay home. He was disappointed but when he went outside, he found some large coins lying on their sidewalk. He said that he felt angels had put them there. He happily went to Sabbath School.

Now as an elderly man, around the age of 90, he began to feel the desire to rejoin the Adventist Church. At this time, his daughter Carol, called me and explained the story to me. She asked me to visit him and arrange for his baptism. I went to see him and found him to be a very warm, friendly person. But it was getting harder for him to get around and his sight and hearing were not real good. Still his desire for baptism was strong. I visited him a number of times to go over the teachings of the church. He hadn't forgotten much. One of his sons began bringing him to church.

So I set a Sabbath afternoon when we would perform the baptismal service. I like to highlight baptism more by doing a separate service for it. The whole church and Carol were there to show their joy and support. Lewis shared with them some of his story, a man coming back home. We sang some joyful hymns together, and then the deacons helped to get him down into the baptismal tank. I praised the Lord for his decision and took him under the water. I'll never forget the happy, broad smile he had when he came up out of the water. He was home again.

Lewis attended only a few more Sabbaths. It got to the point he couldn't stay in his home anymore because of his health (he had been living alone) and so his family put him in a nursing home. This furthered his decline, and in a few more months I was having his funeral. But I was so glad to be a help to him before he died. I'm sure Lewis will have that same happy, broad smile when Jesus calls him forth on the Resurrection Day. He and all that I baptized were divine interventions into my life, as well as theirs.

My second favorite ministerial privilege is to perform weddings. The first one that I conducted by myself was in 2002 while still in our first district. I wasn't ordained yet but the Pennsylvania Conference gave me special permission to perform the wedding. A church member, Dean, who had lost his wife, was planning to marry an Adventist lady, Jennie, who had lost her husband. They came to me like two teenagers wanting to know if I would marry them. It almost seemed like infatuation. But over time, as I talked with them, I could tell they were serious. So we planned a pretty grand affair. And later, as I performed the marriage, I was nearly as happy as they were. To bring two people together in marriage before God is an awesome (divine) experience. And to share the marriage vows with them is a wonderful reminder of our own commitment to our spouse. Dean and Jennie continue to to this day to have a happy, close-knit marriage.

My second opportunity to perform a wedding was for my youngest son, Travis, shortly after I was ordained. I was ordained at the Pennsylvania Conference camp meeting in 2005, another divine intervention for me. I praise God and the Pennsylvania Conference for this special induction into His service, and I was humbled to have this privilege. Betty needs a lot of credit for this milestone, because she was beside me all the way. And she was given the opportunity to stand with me during the ordination, as were the wives of the other candidates.

Travis' wedding was to be at Southern Adventist University near Chattanooga, Tennessee, where both he and his fiancée, Cesilia, had graduated years before. They were merely acquaintances during their school years, but after going their separate ways for several years, they reconnected in a friendship that developed into true love. They were both now living and working near the university and active in a large church close by, so to be invited to perform the wedding was to me a high honor.

The chapel was filled with beautiful flowers and beautiful music. The young couple looked beautiful, as well as the members of their "court". Their pastor was asked to have the opening welcome, and he did real well. And the Lord gave me composure to share a brief message on the "10 commandments" for a good marriage. Then the personal vows they had prepared were shared and soon the introduction of "Mr. and Mrs. Travis Dean" was made. I breathed a sigh of relief and thanksgiving that all had gone well. The Lord was definitely present and made it a divine blessing to me. Travis and Cesilia continue to have a close-knit marriage also and two beautiful children, as well.

They say when you're having fun, time flies quickly. By the summer of 2007 I had turned 65 and had already served five years in the district. It seemed to have gone so quickly. I was now starting to think about retirement. I never really thought I would reach this age. I was sure, when I was baptized 34 years earlier, that Jesus would come before I would retire. But obviously the signs of His coming are much more apparent now than then. One of these signs I refer to is the gospel going to the whole world, and then the end shall come. (Matt 24:14) Today, the gospel is being taken much more fully to the ends of the earth. The Christian media (satellite, TV, radio, Internet) and thousands of missionaries are truly taking it everywhere.

Betty and I even had the privilege of going to a distant land to share the gospel in 2004. We went with a group of gospel workers to Guyana (northern South America). Preparations had been made for us each to hold an evangelistic series in a different town. Betty and I were assigned to a town called Linden. This was a real challenge for me, preaching for the first time with the use of power point and doing it night after night. I prayed a lot that the Holy Spirit would fill me and use me. I spent the day preparing for the meeting to be held that night. One good thing was that I didn't need an interpreter; they speak English there, though a different dialect. The meetings were held in a large outdoor tent. Betty was my assistant, giving basic health talks before my presentations. We had 100 or more who attended. They were attentive and enjoyed learning more of God's Word.

At the close there were 20 who gave their heart to Jesus and were baptized in a nearby river. I felt very blessed by God. These people were choosing eternal life. We had made good friendships in just three weeks. It was a little sad to have to leave. One mother asked if we would bring back her daughter so she could get a better education and start in life. It was tempting but we said "no". I was also asked by some members if I would accept a church district nearby, along a large river. They had an empty church manse (on stilts) for my use and a boat to get around the district. With luscious fruit growing everywhere, that was tempting too. I smiled and said "maybe when I retire".

Well, here I was in 2007 now thinking about retirement already (but not seriously in Guyana). I learned that to get full Social Security benefits I would have to work until I was 10 months past 65. But Betty and I had to start making plans now.

Chapter 18

Retired—Really?

We have 3 children with families whom we love equally and they have always lived far apart. It's strange that children in even close-knit families will end up living all over the country. Work opportunities and marrying someone out of state are big factors. I, of course, had my first job take me to North Carolina, and then I, too, married someone out of state. But still, it seems to be a natural part of our society to leave our roots. I believe that in the process we leave a lot of good family support behind too, especially the grandparents' influence. My children very much enjoyed my parents and kept up a good relationship with them. But we normally only visited them twice a year. But my mother was a good letter writer through the years to all the family. Birthdays were never forgotten.

In 2007 we had our daughter, Renée, and A.J. with 4 children living in Rocky Mount, VA; our son, Shaun, and Aurora with three children living in Orlando, FL; and Travis and Cesilia with one child living near Chattanooga. We hadn't seen any of them very often over the past 12 years, and had missed a lot of birthdays and graduations. So it was hard to decide where we would retire the next year. But, with prayer, we finally decided to move to the Rocky Mount area. Renée had received the least of our time to date and the weather was more moderate there. Plus, Betty's brother, John, and his wife, Sally, were now living on the 15 acres they had purchased from us long ago at our Boones Mill farm. They had been away a long time while John was studying to become a medical doctor, specializing in preventive medicine.

He was now the director of the Rocky Mount Lifestyle Health Center that he and the church had worked together to start. There was some hope among us that we might give them some help, especially in their on-going CHIP (Coronary Heart Improvement Project) seminars. These seminars include 16 group-support classes that teach and train individuals to move toward a plant-based diet. Phenomenal improvements have occurred in people's health in just eight weeks. Cholesterol, triglycerides, blood pressure, blood sugar, and weight all go down significantly for those who follow the program well.

During the summer of 2007 we visited Renée's family and, with much prayer, also began looking at homes and property for sale. We were debt-free now, but we didn't have much in savings to buy anything else. We wanted a place in the country with a few acres and partially wooded. Shortly before returning to Pennsylvania we agreed to buy (on time) a 9-acre all-wooded tract on the rural western edge of the county. We decided we would cut out our own open area. This location was to be significant in the Lord's future work for us after we retired.

Sometime that same summer we announced to our churches that we would be retiring on May 15, 2008. It wasn't an easy announcement to share with them because I knew they would miss us and we would miss them. We were a part of their family and spent a lot of time in their homes. Now it seemed we had decided to break away. But this wasn't to be until "next year", so we all tried to continue on as usual. However, every holiday or annual event that came along, we knew it would be the last one together. I kept telling myself that it was the right thing to do because the district (and the conference) needed younger energetic men, and we needed to spend more time with our grandkids.

Time came, all too soon, for us to say our goodbyes and move south. We would miss our comfortable little home in Pleasantville. The home had been on the market already several months. We had few people looking at it. The economic downturn in our country was already gaining momentum. The only interest seemed to be from a couple who were currently renting, but had good employment. We had gotten to know the wife well through the Lunch Box and Book Bag café. But when we left Pennsylvania, they seemed to have withdrawn their interest. We still thought they were the couple God had planned to buy it. It was the right location for them, the type of house they would like, and it was affordable for them.

In Virginia, we moved into a nice little duplex in Rocky Mount on a six-month lease. We were giving ourselves just six months to clear a site and get a home set up. I guess we function best on deadlines. From the start we seemed to spend all our time cutting up fallen trees for our home site in the daytime, and taking part in a CHIP seminar in the evening.

One experience from our tree cutting work stands out in my mind. One hot day we had a large pile of brush in a pretty safe area that we decided to burn. The pile burned real hot for awhile and then it died down. I then shoveled some dirt on it to cool it down before we left. It was safe even though it had a few wisps of smoke coming up yet. The next day when we returned, we found a note in a zip-lock bag with a rock in it. It was from our neighbor that we hadn't met yet. She reprimanded us for doing our burning on a "dangerous day" and then leaving before the fire was out. One could have said "that's her opinion" and not bothered to pursue it any further. But the Lord impressed us to go visit her and to apologize for our "misdeeds". She (Joyce) responded in a very pleasant, understanding way and soon became a valuable friend to us. It was a lesson to remember: "A soft answer turneth away wrath" (Proverbs 15:1). It's amazing how much an apology in person will defuse an angry attitude.

Betty and I worked hard that summer. We piled small branches in different places out of the way, and for the rest of the tree, we cut it in lengths and stacked them into "teepees" (to dry for firewood), except for the bigger trunk logs. These bigger logs were dragged to the side for cutting into lumber later on. By fall we were able to get the grading done, the septic put in, and the well drilled. We paid for all this by pulling our conference retirement IRA money out just before it took a big plunge. God was still intervening at just the right time for us. When this work was done, we still had a limited amount of cash to buy a mobile home to put on this property. And we had to do it in short order before cold weather set in.

We began by looking at used mobile homes in the 2-county area. We got a little discouraged at what we could get with the money we had on hand. It was then that an Adventist friend told us about a mobile home just ready to go up for sale on the very same road our property was on. After he gave us the telephone number, we called and set up a time we could see it. It was only a mile down the road! The price was right and by far the most for our money. It was an older mobile home, but in very good condition, and a nicely designed one. It looked better than newer used ones we had seen. There was also a 12'x12' solid oak shed that could go with the mobile home for a modest price. They were planning to advertise them in the paper the next week, but we told the lady she wouldn't need to – we would take it! The mobile home mover soon squeezed both the mobile home and the shed into our prepared lot; we had cut no more trees than we absolutely had to. We thanked the Lord again for His providential leading.

Our new home was debt free too!

    We liked our new home from the beginning. I called it "Our Nook in the Woods". It was a down-size to be sure, the home was 14'x 66'. But the setting was peaceful and natural. From the breakfast table we could easily see nature in action. I had never wanted to live in a mobile home permanently, but somehow this arrangement seemed satisfactory. In the late fall I completed the skirting of the home and did some needed insulation. I also planted some flower bulbs to come up in the spring.

    When spring did arrive, I was "planting up a storm". I bought a few plants in town, but most of my plants and seeds were starts from other peoples' gardens. I found out soon that Joyce was a master gardener who not only loved to show her flowers, but also loved to share her flowers. She wouldn't just invite me to come and get some starts; she would actually drive her little tractor and wagon over with a load of plants to give me. And with mulching and watering (and her good advice) I soon had plants everywhere. And she was pleased to see it prosper. The Lord is so good to us!

    Shortly after we arrived from Pennsylvania, we began to get acquainted with our pastor, Kevin, a very likeable man. He had a 4-church district that was quite spread out. I didn't envy him at all. He seemed to want to put us to work as soon as we had settled in the duplex. Of course, that's a good step for a pastor to take when a recently retired pastor moves into his area. From the start he wanted to know if we would be willing to help out in one of his four churches, in Stuart, VA. It was about 30 minutes from our mobile home, on into the next county. We agreed to visit some and consider it. Pastor Kevin also wanted us to work together to form a Bible study group in our new home from interests that he knew that lived in our area. For various reasons this study group just didn't work out. The Lord will sometimes close a good door to lead you to another one that He has in mind.

    So we began to focus more on the Stuart Church. It had only

about 10 members attending most Sabbaths, but they were very friendly and hospitable. They hoped we would make it our home church. Betty and I have always felt missionary minded to some degree, and, after a few visits, this seemed to us to be a good missionary field. When the church had been built, it was right on busy state highway 58 about six miles west of Stuart. Then later, the highway was straightened and this put the church out of sight on a short dead-end road. Church membership had declined since then, partly due to a new church plant spawned by previous members of the Stuart congregation. The remaining members were now older but still very faithful stewards. So with this challenge lying before us, we decided to join the church. We believed that "with God nothing shall be impossible" (Luke 1:37).

This promise in Luke was also true of our house in Pennsylvania. Our realtor in Pleasantville had been working diligently trying to sell our empty home. The fall of 2008 had proved fruitless for her and now the cold winter was on in that area. In December the same couple that had shown interest before we left came back to talk about our home again. Knowing the state of the economy, they were trying to find out how low we might be willing to go on our price. We responded by saying we thought the house was well-priced already and we weren't willing to drop significantly. It seemed that the husband was still interested but the wife wasn't. Then, in January the husband contacted our realtor again. This time an agreement was worked out with a little give and take. We were so grateful to the Lord that we could sell the house, and in January 2009, no less. An empty distant house in the winter using utilities is a burden and a worry. So I again can say "with God nothing shall be impossible".

Back in the summer of 2008 Pastor Kevin had arranged for an academy-age youth group to spend a few weeks of their summer selling Christian literature in our Stuart area. Betty and I were there when they had a special Sabbath morning service at the church just before they left. They were excited about some of the nice visits they had been having and the books they had sold. The girls and the guys all gave a special testimony of God's leading. I was asked by Pastor Kevin to make a friendly visit in the fall to see how the people were enjoying their purchases and to see if we could help in any other way.

    I enjoyed meeting quite a few of their contacts. One family lived on a quiet residential street in Stuart in a nice older home. There I met Sam and Pat, grandparents to an 8-year old girl and a 3-year old boy. The mother of the two children had actually bought the books, but I had a warm spiritual visit with Sam and Pat. He had some interest in Bible teachings concerning the last days before Jesus comes. They both asked me to come back with Betty sometime. As I left that day I noticed a "For Sale" sign in front of the large house across the street. The house was old but beautiful. It had a long wrap-around front porch with big white pillars to go with it. There were large healthy maple trees in the front yard. To me, it looked like a colonial plantation home. I thought to myself that somebody wealthy can sure get a nice home there.

    My next visit later in the fall was by myself again. I had a good visit; Pat and Sam were retired too and a few years older than I was. They were attending a very large Pentecostal church outside of town. He shared a lot of their past, hardships and good times, and how they ended up in Stuart. On my 3rd visit, in the winter, Betty went with me and we discovered that Pat was in the nursing home recovering from a fall in which she had broken a leg. One of their cats had tripped her up. We went to see her that day and had a very nice visit and prayer with her. I also had noticed that day that the big colonial home was still for sale. I told Betty that was the house of my dreams. "I wonder what it costs." She checked online and discovered it would need to remain just a dream.

    We were gone a lot the next couple months to visit both boys and their families and to attend a funeral in Missouri for Betty's sister. In late April Betty and I went back to visit Pat and Sam. It was fun to see them again. The colonial house was still for sale, with a "reduced price" notice attached to it. When we got home, we checked the current listed price. It had dropped a lot, but was still out of our range. Later, we asked Sam about it. He said "You don't want to buy that house; it has problems!" The 2nd owner back had wrecked the house. She had bought the house with money gained from her husband's death while serving in Iraq. But she was bipolar and it seemed she'd been quite disturbed from this loss and had tried to cover up her sorrow with a wild life.

Sam said a lady living in Florida had bought the house at a low price planning to restore it. Her college age son was given the responsibility of doing much of the work. This didn't work out to her satisfaction; it seems her son was bipolar too. And he also liked to party; cops were often called. However, some good work had been done downstairs, but nothing upstairs yet. The owner was now seeing it as a poor investment and just wanted to sell it. I began to think that it would at least be nice to see the house.

So in early June, we arranged with the realtor, Karen, to walk through the house. It was awesome to me when I first stepped in the door. The large foyer had dark wainscot on all the walls, 4 feet up from the floor, as well as on the large open stairway going to the second floor. Then there was more beautiful wainscot in the large living room and dining room. The living room also had a large fireplace with gas logs and built-in book shelves on each side that matched the wainscot. Ceilings were, of course, high and they had beautiful multiple lamps. All these rooms were already nicely furnished. There was a small butler pantry going toward the kitchen. The kitchen was a good size, with all appliances, an island and a large food pantry. On the same floor was also a central bathroom, a large bedroom with a fireplace and its own bathroom, a back dining area, and a back stairway to the upstairs.

All that needed done downstairs was to refinish a couple floors and paint the bedroom and its bathroom, and it would be complete. But the upstairs looked like it had gone through a war. All the floors were ugly and dirty where carpet had been pulled up. Some ceilings were caving in. All walls needed repaired and painted. Two outside walls needed to be repaired because of roof leaks that still needed repair. There was daylight through some of the outside walls. Several of the windows were in need of being replaced. Betty was figuring in her head what the cost would be for all this needed repair; I was picturing in my mind what all this would look like with a skilled worker and a lot of my hard labor. One of the assets we saw upstairs was a large beautiful king-size bed with high posts.

There was also a 20x40 in-ground swimming pool in the backyard with a diving board and a lot of nice decking going to it. But this pool, too, scared people because it was empty, unkempt and dirty. It needed paint too. The little water in it housed frogs and mosquitoes. What expenditure would this take? Would it even hold water?

We told the realtor, Karen, we would pray about it. If we were going to buy a house in the Stuart area, Betty wanted to compare this house with some alternative housing possibilities. She called on some advertisements for homes and we looked at one or two. Then we looked at the big house again. Betty was even more hesitant this time, just like other lookers were. Without her support, I reluctantly agreed that we would decline to make an offer. I knew that if it was the Lord's will, we would be in agreement. The work would require our mutual efforts too.

Somewhere about this time I got a call from friends in Pennsylvania wanting our opinion on some work and housing decisions they were currently faced with. I felt impressed to tell them that there was a job opening at the Rocky Mount Lifestyle Center (which they would enjoy) and that we had a mobile home that they could possibly rent, should we move to Stuart. They said it sounded providential to them (and to me). They would pray about it and call back.

Meanwhile Betty was having second thoughts about being the one to spoil my dream. She would rather have the Lord cancel the dream. In talking with Karen again, she informed us that the owner was planning to put in central air in the home (at a cost of $20,000), hoping it would sell better. So Karen said we could tell her not to do that and submit a bid of $20,000 less. This was getting us closer to what we could afford. So Betty (and the bank) helped me figure what we could afford to borrow, and what our down payment could be and still have enough funds to hopefully repair the upstairs.

Doing this we came up with an offer even lower than Karen was suggesting. But this is all that we could afford. And our offer included all the furnishings, which the owner was offering to sell separately for $5,000. Karen forwarded our offer, and later called back saying the owner would accept the offer, but would not include the furnishings. We replied that it had to include the furnishings too. We were holding to our offer because this was the point we were making our "fleece" before the Lord, to say yes or no. It wasn't long until Karen called back to say the owner had said "Yes". Exactly one month later the loan and paper work was signed and the house was ours. I had to admit to Betty and others that we were again stepping out in faith. So I want to share how the Lord again intervened, stretching our dollars, guiding in the work to be done, and opening opportunities to serve Him.

Chapter 19

A New Challenge

The month after we purchased our house, Lois and Larry arrived to visit and to check on the job opening. In a couple days Lois was hired as a manager at the Lifestyle Center. They then decided to rent our mobile home. This gave us a little more breathing room in our budget. They also decided to join our Stuart Church. Their singing and music abilities have been a real asset to our church worship and outreach. They lead in our singing once a month at the local nursing home in town. And Lois and Larry have both been a rich blessing to the Lifestyle Center's work in Rocky Mount as well. We thank the Lord for sending them our way.

The real key to renovating the upstairs of our new home would be finding the right skilled worker(s) to do the work we couldn't do. Being new to the county we called different contractors and asked them to give us a bid on all or parts of the work to be done. We talked to several men that were experienced in home renovations. They seemed ready to work, but they each, for some reason, never replied with a bid. It seemed strange.

I began quickly with things I could do. I sanded and refinished two floors downstairs before we moved in. I spent days cutting back the heavy growth of vines, shrubs, and bushes around the house. Our new neighbors, Asaph and Elvira, helped us to empty out the dirty water and the frogs from the pool with buckets. I gave some of the frogs a new home in the Mayo River. We used buckets because the pool had no way to drain the water out the bottom. Asaph had recently retired, at 80, and they were planning to move back to their home in Canada. So they had their house up for sale. We knew when they did move, we would miss their hospitality and helpfulness.

We were there but a short time when the sewage line to the street plugged up. We hired a man with a roto-rooter to clear it out. The next day we found out we had a plugged line below the kitchen, probably from the previous day's work. So I called an Adventist plumber from the Rocky Mount church. He said he was busy but he recommended that we call his son, Jeff, who needed work and would be able to handle it. Jeff came the same day and cut the pipe, cleaned it out and repaired it very economically.

We then proceeded to show him the house and the work that needed done. He told us he had done similar work with his dad on big homes in Connecticut and would be glad to help us out. It turned out Jeff was a God-send to us. He was skilled, innovative and he knew the "tricks of the trade" in working with an old house like ours. He and I worked so well together. I did all the work on the floors, the painting, and insulation and Jeff did the skilled work of replacing 2 ceilings, repairing an outer wall, and doing electrical and plumbing work. And Jeff's pay was very reasonable, making our money stretch farther. He would also use materials that we had in our shed as much as he could.

The floors upstairs first needed to be cleaned of glue and dirt before I could even start sanding. We (Betty did one room) used Acetone and a wide wood chisel for this cleaning; this was days of work. Then I rented a sander, one day for each room. Then came the tedious job of using a hand sander to do the corners, around the pipes, and all the dips in the floor that couldn't be done with the large sander. But I was greatly encouraged because the wood that finally came up was a beautiful hard pine with gorgeous configurations. This was the prettiest flooring I had ever seen. No one could have known this as they walked through the house. Only the Lord knew the beauty that was underneath. (Jesus also looks at people the same way: "There's a beauty there if they would only let Me do the work.") Finally, I used 4-5 coats of Lowe's Varathane polyurethane to cover each floor. What a change was taking place!

Betty and I then had the joy of picking out different pastel colors for each room and the hallway that would accent the floor. When the ceiling and walls were painted, it was amazing to see how it brightened up these big rooms. It made us want to start on another room. This took months because I did all the painting by myself to save money. We got insulation blown into the attic. And I spent days putting more insulation underneath the house and more days insulating cracks in the house. And we could feel the difference. I didn't work very many long days; I tried to pace myself. Jeff was able to come regularly on the days that we needed him. He enjoyed being a part of the renovation.

It was amazing what time, work, a modest amount of money, and God's wisdom could do to change the appearance of the second floor. I'll never forget those two years and how everything just seemed to fall in place. For example, we needed a mantle for the upstairs fireplace. We checked a store in Roanoke with a large selection but we couldn't find what we wanted. I checked with a local antique and craft store. They had one the size we needed for $69. It had one fixable flaw and needed refinished. As I was looking it over the man said "I'll let you have it for half the price". I thanked him and told him I would buy it. Jeff fixed the flaw and I refinished it and it looks great.

The windows of the house, as you might guess, are also on

the large size. There were 14 that needed replaced. A window company in nearby Martinsville advertised one price for any size window replacement. We ordered all 14 from them. As they were replacing the 5 windows in the upstairs day room, they discovered the wall structure needed repaired before they could put the new windows in. Most window companies would have said "when you get the wall repaired, we'll come back and put your windows in". But these men were also good carpenters. They said they would go ahead and fix it for only a modest additional cost. Some of the wood for doing it came from my shed, a lot of which was left from the previous owner. God is so good!

I also painted the large, 2-story shed in the back. It was flaking badly. I spent hours scraping it, and then gave it a primer and a top coat using paint that had been left in the shed. It looks like a new shed. And for the swimming pool I filled in some cracks on the floor and painted it a nice blue. The question still remained as to whether it would hold the water when full. We happen to have a fire hydrant on our side of the street, so the town manager said they would fill it up for us for a little over $100. We agreed and found that the pool held its water. We, family, and friends have enjoyed hours of relaxing and swimming in it.

As big as the house is (3680 sq. ft.) it is an easy one to get on the roof and once there the roof isn't very steep. I thank the Lord for this because I've had to go on the roof many times to clean gutters, repair leaks, and to repaint the roof. But now we can rest well on a stormy night. I got good advice on the roof work and other work from the manager of the local hardware store, a great guy.

The roof work reminds me of an ice storm that occurred while we were away for a few days. We have a few large white pines at the back of the house. The trunk of one is only 20 feet from the house and some of the limbs hang out over the roof. (However, I've cut some of them back while standing on the roof.) The ice from the freezing rain built up on the limbs and some of the large limbs began breaking off. But not one of the limbs hit the house itself! There was a whole pile of limbs on the ground, which I had to use a chain saw to cut up. God's angels surely watched over our home while we were away.

Our home was never meant to be for just Betty and me. It was, most of all, meant to serve the community and the church. Although we have set it up as an official bed and breakfast (B&B) facility, we have promoted it as a lifestyle B&B. We encourage people to come who need some marital support, rest and relaxation, or help in improving their diet and lifestyle. Betty enjoys giving cooking demonstrations and sharing recipes. We have professional videos and DVDs for visitors' use as well. And we share from our own experience and learning. We've had different ones coming for this purpose, but we've also enjoyed meeting wonderful people who come just to stay a night or two as B&B guests.

For our 40th wedding anniversary we decided to have an Open House on a Sunday afternoon in May 2012. I wanted us and our church to get acquainted with more people in the area. I invited neighbors, friends, our family, and church families to come and enjoy music, singing, refreshments, and good fellowship. Our local church bought flowers and helped with the refreshments. I had selected photos of our family over our 40 years and laid them out for people to see. I wanted to uplift marriage and family and I pray it did. We had a large puzzle for people to relax and work on. I had invited some talented musicians and singers to come and they produced some lovely, spiritual music that inspired everyone. The 2:00 – 5:00 p.m. hours planned extended well into the evening. It was a foretaste of heaven.

Our home has also been a great help to our church. We've been involved in the church move, moving from the country into town. The planning began about a year after we started attending Stuart. We've used our house for lots of meetings and gatherings during this process. The church decided to move when it was given the opportunity to sell their building to the Virginia Department of Transportation (VDOT). VDOT was going to need the land in its future widening of Route 58 west of town. In January 2010 we sold the church to VDOT at a fair price and in June we bought a building in town.

The building is 5000 square feet and had once been a Sears catalogue store. When we bought it, it was a solid, rectangular, metal frame building that was completely gutted. Good insulation was still on all outer walls and the ceiling, and the fixtures still in place for plumbing and electric. The building has a solid block wall dividing the interior into 2/3 and 1/3 sections. The smaller part, we decided, would be for a community service center. There is still a nice paved parking lot in the front. The building is located on a well-traveled street. The lot is one acre in size.

A really nice benefit to us was that VDOT has a policy that when a church or organization has to sell its building to them, they will give financial aid in the renovation of another building that is purchased. The maximum help they give is $25,000 in matching funds spent on renovation. This was the amount our church received. VDOT also permitted us to remain in our old church free of charge until we received our occupancy permit for the church sanctuary. This was much longer than the normal limit. God has been extra good to us in our relationship with VDOT.

The sanctuary and bathrooms (phase 1 of our renovation) look great now. Our former pews fit perfectly in our new sanctuary. And this wasn't planned by the architect. (I'm sorry Pastor Kevin didn't get to preach there. On August 1 he took a call to Ouachita Hills Academy in Arkansas, just at the time we were getting our occupancy.) We've since had a new front entrance built at the middle door area that has helped spruce up the outer look of our building. A friend of ours from our first church district in Pennsylvania, who now works at Indiana Academy, has come twice with several students to work on the Sabbath School classrooms, kitchen, and fellowship room areas. They do this as a missionary and training project. So God has immensely blessed us through them as well. Betty and I housed and fed them and really enjoyed getting to know the students.

As we later, hopefully soon, complete the community service section, I'm looking forward to how the Lord leads and blesses in our choice of outreach to the community. In the mean time, Betty and I have personally enjoyed getting involved in various town and county activities ourselves. The one I've enjoyed most has been my ministry time at the local jail. I spend my time there sharing experiences that show how much God loves individual people, including them, and how he wants to change their lives to be happy and productive. I really count it a privilege and a divine providence that I can be there.

I share with the inmates some of the same personal experiences that I have shared in this book. I also share stories from the Bible that show God manifesting His great love for individuals and His power to change lives. And then, lastly, I share similar providential experiences from more modern times that I've gathered from my years in ministry. It's amazing how the inmates enjoy my sharing stories of God intervening in people's lives. It seems to make God more real and personal to them. They seem eager to know more about this loving Saviour and to gain similar experiences. And some of them are doing just that!

I also enjoy very much working with our local church. We're small but we're taking on big challenges. I've been volunteering as pastor during the ten months that we've been without one. I also help the Martinsville Adventist church nearby. It's a good time to be preaching the love of Jesus and about Him being the only real hope we have in today's world.

Probably Betty's favorite community outreach is working with the local hospice group that crochets and knits prayer shawls and other items for hundreds of people in the area. It is a very friendly group of ladies. At Christmas they joined together in making hundreds of cookies for hospice patients. Betty loves to crochet and recently has relearned knitting. She gets some crocheting time in while she volunteers once a week as a pink lady at the local hospital gift shop. She is always making a hat, neck scarf, head band, or other item for friends and family, especially grandchildren.

Betty also volunteers at the Presbyterian Church's used clothing store. It's a nice way to get to know the people in Stuart. They are friendly, country people. She occasionally shares some Adventist literature there.

Chapter 20

Closing Thoughts

God can do (and is doing) amazing things in our world today. The world is so full of Satan's evil, destructive work that it is only natural that God, too, would manifest Himself in loving, powerful ways. Everyone in the world must choose whom they will serve before Jesus comes, either our God of love and righteousness or Satan with his selfish and evil ways. Joshua stated the issue clearly to the Israelites after they had entered the Promised Land. He said "choose you this day whom you will serve, whether the gods which your fathers served … or the gods of the Amorites …, but as for me and my house, we will serve the Lord". (Joshua 24:15)

Jesus is doing everything He can to draw us to Him. But He will not take away our choice to decide for ourselves. Every individual is vitally important to Him; you are important to Him. If He can't reach your heart through the Bible, or through nature, or through spiritual music, He will try to reach you through a Christian's life or testimony or by He Himself intervening in your life to show you there is a better, happier way of living than what the world offers. God went to great lengths, using all the above, to reach my heart.

Closing Thoughts // 125

Jesus covers all the bases for our salvation. He is our Creator, Redeemer, Sustainer, Provider, Friend, Mediator, Advocate, and coming King. But Satan has so clouded people's thinking today that God still has to miraculously intervene in their lives to show them that He wants to be the Lord of their life. Sports and amusements, stressful work, family problems, and the love of money all tend to shut Jesus out of our every day life. But God won't give up on us until we clearly and finally say no to Him.

In John 14:3 Jesus clearly says He will come again. We don't know exactly when that will be, but Bible predictions declare this won't be long. Paul says in 1 Thessalonians 4:16, 17 that when Jesus does come "He will descend from heaven with a shout, with the voice of the archangel, and with the trump of God: and the dead in Christ shall rise first: then we which are alive and remain shall be caught up together with them in the clouds, to meet the Lord in the air: and so shall we ever be with the Lord." What a glorious day, and what a glorious future! We mustn't miss out.

My encouragement to you is to come to know the Lord. He is an awesome, loving God. David came to know the Lord well. He describes Him in Psalms 86:15: "But thou, O Lord, art a God full of compassion, and gracious, longsuffering, and plenteous in mercy and truth." He is this and more. Paul says in Romans 2:4 that as we come to know the goodness of God, it will lead us to repentance. And repentance leads us to salvation.

The wonderful thing about beginning a walk with Jesus is that He will manifest Himself to you along the way to assure you that you are on the right path. Through the Bible, prayer, nature, and His personal interventions He will make Himself known to you more and more. And He will begin to disclose to you avenues of service that He wants you to take that will make your life more satisfying and purposeful. God will also give you new talents (spiritual gifts) that will enable you to do new work that you once thought you would never do. I can vouch for this. As a young man I never dreamed I would be a Christian salesman, a baker, or a pastor. But I enjoyed them all because I was where the Lord wanted me to be. This is the key to happiness, being where the Lord wants you to be.

So, I hope I've given you some food for thought, some ideas to try, and some courage to step out in faith into the wonderful world of serving our Lord. May the Lord appear more appealing to you. Psalms 34:8 says "O taste and see that the Lord is good: blessed is the man that trusteth in Him." And may you enjoy the divine interventions that He manifests in your life.

We invite you to view the complete
selection of titles we publish at:

www.AspectBooks.com

Scan with your mobile
device to go directly
to our website.

Please write or email us your praises, reactions, or
thoughts about this or any other book we publish at:

P.O. Box 954
Ringgold, GA 30736

info@AspectBooks.com

Aspect Books titles may be purchased in bulk for
educational, business, fund-raising, or sales promotional use.
For information, please e-mail:

BulkSales@AspectBooks.com

Finally, if you are interested in seeing
your own book in print, please contact us at:

publishing@AspectBooks.com

We would be happy to review your manuscript for free.

www.ingramcontent.com/pod-product-compliance
Lightning Source LLC
Chambersburg PA
CBHW062012180426

43199CB00034B/2526